# WINE BITES

# WINE BITES

## SIMPLE MORSELS THAT PAIR PERFECTLY WITH WINE

*by* Barbara Scott-Goodman

*Photographs* by Kate Mathis

**CHRONICLE BOOKS**

SAN FRANCISCO

Library of Congress Cataloging-in-Publication Data available.

ISBN 978-0-8118-7630-8

Manufactured in China

Designed by Barbara Scott-Goodman

Food styling by Adrienne Anderson

Prop styling by Marcus Hay

10 9 8 7 6 5 4 3 2 1

Chronicle Books LLC

680 Second Street

San Francisco, CA  94107

www.chroniclebooks.com

# contents

## chapter 6 • **fried bites:** decadent, crunchy bites that are finger-licking good

## chapter 7 • **seafood:** savory & scrumptious fish & shellfish bites

## chapter 8 • **meats:** hearty bites & more to serve with good wine

## chapter 9 • **small sweets & treats:** delicious last bites & sips of the evening

# introduction

Whenever life gives you cause for celebration, throw a party! Any reason will do: the arrival of summer, a promotion, your kid got a job. The important thing is to share the good times with your friends. Gatherings that bring good company make our long days worthwhile, raise our spirits, and enhance our lives. So why not invite your friends over, open a few bottles of wine, and have a little get-together?

Whether you're having a few friends in for a convivial glass of wine before heading out to dinner or you're hosting an extravagant cocktail party, your guests will want something to eat while toasting, sipping, and chatting. Offer them some delectable snacks to nibble on with their drinks—a beloved combination that deliciously lends itself to the name of "wine bites." These are zesty finger foods: delicious, imaginative, and easy to eat with wineglass in hand. Set out bowls of homemade spiced popcorn and nuts and marinated olives, and serve a variety of snacks like Stilton-Stuffed Dates with Prosciutto (page 44), classic Gougères (page 46); homemade pizzas (pages 61 to 67); toothsome toast creations like Bruschetta with Figs, Prosciutto & Arugula (page 77); and crisp, earthy fried Egg-plant Chips (page 98). Entice your guests with piquant seafood dishes like Ginger Shrimp Cocktail with Spicy Dipping Sauce (page 102) and Chilled Mussels Vinaigrette (page 107) and savory two- or three-bite meat dishes such as Cumin-Scented Lamb Kebabs (page 135); Mini Empanadas with Beef, Green Olives & Raisins (page 133); and Pulled Pork

Sliders (page 139). Cheese plates that include a range of well-chosen international and domestic cheeses, accompanied by colorful fresh and dried fruit, are lovely to serve; and cheese pairs beautifully with almost all styles of wine. The same goes for sumptuous antipasto platters, tapas spreads, and charcuterie boards. These plates, which are easy and fun to assemble, can be as simple and casual or as elaborate and abundant as you wish. All of these dishes can be eaten with fingers, toothpicks, or skewers. And above all, they'll be consumed with delight.

*Wine Bites* is full of scrumptious recipes and innovative ideas that will inspire you to throw a festive bash with ease. It can be a surprisingly low-key effort to gather your friends and family together and enjoy the simple pleasures of eating good food and drinking good wine. Nevertheless, there are recipes here that cover a range of visions—big cocktail party buffets as well as intimate get-togethers in the kitchen—and don't all good parties end up in the kitchen? You can mix and match recipes from every chapter and create your own menus, from simple snacks that can be easily made with on-hand pantry items to more complex dishes that may require a bit more prep and cooking time.

What is most important is that your party is embarked upon with a sense of fun and warmth and a spirit of generosity. Now, don't you feel like celebrating?

# stocking the pantry

*A well-stocked pantry, a few refrigerator staples, and a corner of your freezer can contain everything you need to put together a delicious, varied, and attractive menu of hors d'oeuvres and small bites ranging from sweet to savory, hearty to light, to complement wines of every color and style. And when you're well supplied with staples, a single stop at your butcher, fishmonger, or greengrocer can fill out a wonderful spread for a brunch, lunch, or dinner party.*

## the pantry

The list of basics in the pantry arsenal starts with good-quality extra-virgin olive oil; a vinegar or two (or three) including regular balsamic and white balsamic or champagne vinegar; kosher and sea salts; and fresh black pepper. Be sure to always have Dijon mustard in good supply for vinaigrettes and other sauces, and best-quality mayonnaise for dips and spreads. A store of several kinds of dried and canned beans (think red, white, black,

and chickpea) is indispensable for more dips and spreads; chickpeas are especially versatile on the hors d'oeuvres stage, delicious tossed with almost any combination of herb and spice and roasted until crisp-tender. Beans also add heartiness to salads and make for easy soups, side dishes, and main courses. All of these hardworking pantry staples are essential for everyday cooking as well as for entertaining.

For the next tier in the pantry, savvy hosts know that some very good things do come in cans and jars. Consider the following lists for things to keep in mind (and on hand) for impromptu parties or a spur-of-the moment glass of wine with friends in the kitchen:

• Jarred roasted red peppers, sun-dried tomatoes, and marinated artichoke hearts and canned sardines, octopus, oysters, and anchovies are all excellent, festive bites to serve on crackers, toasts, or thin slices of baguette.

• Good-quality canned tuna is perfect for bruschetta or finger sandwiches; try tossing it with fresh lemon juice and white beans.

• A wide variety of good-quality salsas of every flavor from *verde* to peach and canned dips and spreads such as black bean, tapenade, and caponata now fills the shelves of supermarkets and specialty-food stores, offering a seemingly infinite choice of tasty and easy-to-serve but elegant dips and toppings for taco chips or wedges of pita bread.

• Popcorn and an assortment of nuts such as almonds, pecans, walnuts, peanuts, and pistachios are always good to have on hand. Popcorn sprinkled with sea salt, a classic often relegated to movie time, is actually terrifically satisfying with chilled white wine. Top the hot popped corn with grated Parmesan cheese and bring on the red wine. Serve nuts on their own or toss them with a few spices and olive oil and roast them in the oven.

• Keep a good supply of crackers in the pantry. They are indispensable for serving with spreads and dips and a variety of toppings.

## the refrigerator

The refrigerator is an important extension of your pantry, the place for those items that, while perishable, will keep through several shopping trips—i.e., from 1 week to as much as 3 months.

• Butter will keep in the refrigerator for up to 6 weeks.

• Fresh eggs can be stored in the refrigerator for up to 3 weeks after their "sell by" date.

• Olives packed in oil or brine, cornichons, and other pickles, and pickled or marinated vegetables such as pepperoncini, cauliflower, and green beans will keep, tightly covered in jars or in airtight

*stocking the pantry*  11

containers, for up to 6 months and supply interesting antipasti or add salty, sour, or tangy texture and taste to many mixes and dishes; or serve them on their own in bowls for nibbling.

• Keep a top-quality grating cheese like Parmesan or Asiago on hand; wrap tightly in plastic wrap/cling film or wax/greaseproof paper and store in the cheese drawer of your fridge. They will usually keep for up to 3 to 4 weeks after opening.

• Cream cheese, goat cheese, and feta cheese are also very useful for creating a wide range of wine bites, although they have a shorter shelf life of about 1 to 2 weeks.

• Tubs of freshly made hummus, *baba ganoush*, *taramosalata*, and tzatziki from Middle Eastern and Greek markets are great to have on hand for parties (you can find good packaged versions of these in your supermarket deli section, too). Once opened, they should be used by their "sell by" date.

• If you're feeling extravagant, keep a tin of caviar in the fridge. Fresh caviar can be stored for 2 to 3 weeks. Any uneaten caviar should be covered tightly and consumed within 2 to 3 days. A delicious, less expensive version of caviar is salmon roe or red caviar. It is an essential ingredient in Chopped Egg Salad & Salmon Caviar Toasts (page 112). Dry Champagne or sparkling wine are wonderful to drink with caviar.

• Fresh herbs such as flat-leaf parsley, cilantro/coriander, thyme, rosemary, and mint are very versatile and good to have on hand in the crisper drawer. They add flavor, texture, and visual appeal to dips, spreads, and salsas and are also essential for garnishes.

• Be sure to have lemons and limes in your crisper drawer at all times for bright, super-fresh citrus flavor "on tap."

## the freezer

• Just about any type of bread, such as baguettes, country loaves, rye or pumpernickel bread, or pita, can be frozen. Whether you're freezing a whole loaf, a half loaf, or slices, the bread will keep well as long as it is wrapped and stored properly. Wrap the bread tightly in plastic wrap/cling film, freezer paper, or aluminum foil and store for up to 1 month. To thaw, loosen the wrapping of the bread and let stand at room temperature for 2 to 3 hours. Brush slices of baguette with olive oil and pop them in a 400°F/200°C/gas 6 oven for a few minutes until lightly golden and you have an instant supply of the European-style toasts popularly known as crostini; serve warm or at room temperature with any variety of accompaniments you like. Sprinkle a little grated Parmesan cheese on top of the oil before placing in the oven for Parmesan Toasts (page 80) that are delicious alone as well as with toppings.

• Keep a few bags of homemade or commercial pizza dough on hand in the freezer for impromptu pizza parties and quick dinners or snacks.

• Butter will keep in the freezer for up to 1 year.

• It's a good idea to store nuts and seeds in plastic freezer bags in the freezer to keep them from turning stale or rancid. They thaw very quickly.

• Homemade pesto and tomato sauces made with fresh seasonal produce freeze beautifully. They are welcome in the winter months and make great toppings for crostini or bruschetta.

It only takes a bit of advance planning and some smart grocery shopping to keep your pantry and refrigerator full of goodies ready and waiting for the next party.

*Chapter 1*

# SNACKS, NUTS & OLIVES

TASTY BITE-SIZE TREATS
FOR ALL OCCASIONS

# spiced popcorn & pumpkin seeds

**serves 8 to 10**

This addictive snack is a great combination of spice, salt, and crunch, and awakens the palate perfectly for sips of red or white wine. Set a few bowls around the room when you entertain for easy nibbling, and watch how quickly they empty. Salty snacks like this one and the Piquant Roasted Chickpeas (page 18), Chile-Lime Peanuts (page 20), and Roasted Mixed Nuts (page 21), pair well with light, fruity reds and rosés, and whites such as Chardonnay, Sauvignon Blanc, and Pinot Grigio.

Pumpkin Seeds:
1 tsp salt
½ tsp paprika
Pinch of garlic powder
Pinch of cayenne pepper
Freshly ground black pepper
2 cups/230 g raw hulled pumpkin seeds
1 tbsp olive oil

Popcorn:
3 tbsp corn oil
½ cup/85 g popcorn
Kosher salt

To make the pumpkin seeds: In a small bowl, stir together the salt, paprika, garlic powder, cayenne, and black pepper to taste and set aside.

Combine the pumpkin seeds and olive oil in a large bowl and toss well to coat. Transfer the pumpkin seeds to a large nonstick frying pan and place over high heat. Toast, shaking the pan and tossing the seeds constantly, until browned and puffed, about 5 minutes. Return to the oiled bowl, add the spice mixture, and toss well again to coat evenly.

To make the popcorn: Heat a heavy-bottomed saucepan with a tight-fitting lid over medium heat. Add the corn oil and popcorn and shake the pan to spread the popcorn and oil evenly over the bottom of the pan. Partially cover the pan to allow the steam to escape, and cook the popcorn, constantly shaking the pan, until the popping begins, quickens, and then stops.

Remove from the heat, sprinkle with salt, and toss to coat. Add the popcorn to the bowl with the spiced pumpkin seeds and toss until well combined. Serve at once in a bowl or basket lined with a paper or cloth napkin.

# piquant roasted chickpeas

**serves 6 to 8**

These tasty, savory chickpeas are a snap to make and require nothing more than a few pantry items you should always have on hand: canned chickpeas, olive oil, and spices. The symphony of spices here is well matched with a red wine with lots of fruit, as rich a Chardonnay as you like, or grassy Sauvignon Blancs and Pinot Grigios.

Two 15½-oz/445-g cans chickpeas,
  rinsed and drained
½ tsp paprika
½ tsp ground coriander

½ tsp ground cumin
Pinch of cayenne pepper
3 tbsp olive oil
Kosher salt and freshly ground black pepper

Preheat the oven to 400°F/200°C/gas 6. Put the chickpeas in a large bowl.

In a small bowl, stir together the paprika, coriander, cumin, and cayenne until well mixed. Sprinkle over the chickpeas. Add the olive oil and toss well to coat evenly.

Spread the chickpeas in a single layer on a rimmed baking sheet/tray and sprinkle with salt and black pepper. Roast, stirring occasionally, until the chickpeas are crisp and golden, about 30 minutes.

Remove from the oven and transfer to paper towels/absorbent paper to drain. Let cool completely. Taste and adjust the seasoning, if necessary, and serve.

**Make-Ahead:** The chickpeas can be made up to 4 hours in advance. Store in an airtight container at room temperature.

# sweet & spicy mixed nuts

**serves 6 to 8**

This delicious mix of roasted nuts has a nice salty-sweet coating of sugar, five spice powder, and kosher salt. Try these with Merlot or Cabernet Sauvignon.

2 cups/230 g raw unsalted peanuts,
   pecans, almonds, or cashews,
   or any combination
3 tbsp sugar
2 tbsp five spice powder
1 tbsp corn or canola oil
Kosher salt

Preheat the oven to 350°F/180°C/gas 4.

Put the nuts, sugar, five spice powder, oil, and salt in a large bowl and toss together to coat well.

Spread the nuts in a single layer on a rimmed baking sheet/tray and toast in the oven, shaking the pan occasionally, until the coating is dry and the nuts are lightly browned and fragrant, 15 to 20 minutes. Let cool completely before serving. Season with additional salt, if necessary.

**Make-Ahead:** The nuts will keep in an airtight container for up to 2 weeks. If they lose their crispness, reheat in an oven at 250°F/120°C/gas ½ for about 15 minutes, then let cool.

# chile-lime peanuts

**serves 10 to 12**

Just a touch of lime and salt, mingled with the scent of cumin and the kick of cayenne, elevates everyday peanuts to a sublime snack. Be sure to let the peanuts cool completely before serving. Pair with light, fruity reds and rosés, or any icy cold dry white wine.

| | |
|---|---|
| 4 cups/450 g unsalted peanuts | 1 tsp ground cumin |
| 3 tbsp fresh lime juice | 2 tsp kosher salt |
| 2 tbsp olive oil | 1 tsp cayenne pepper |
| 1 tbsp paprika | |

Preheat the oven to 250°F/120°C/gas ½. Put the peanuts in a large bowl.

In a small bowl, whisk together the lime juice, olive oil, paprika, cumin, salt, and cayenne. Pour the spice mixture over the peanuts and toss well to coat evenly.

Spread the peanuts in a single layer on a rimmed baking sheet/tray and toast in the oven, shaking the pan occasionally, until the coating is dry and the nuts are lightly browned and fragrant, 25 to 30 minutes. Let cool completely before serving.

**Make-Ahead:** The peanuts will keep in an airtight container for up to 2 weeks. If they lose their crispness, reheat in an oven at 250°F/120°C/gas ½ for about 15 minutes, then let cool.

# roasted mixed nuts

**serves 6 to 8**

Blend and toast your spices to give these roasted nuts rich fragrance and flavor. They're always a welcome snack for friends who drop in for a glass of wine. Salt and crunch are pleasantly offset by light reds and dry or semidry whites; also try a buttery Chardonnay to complement the rich oils in the nuts.

½ tsp ground cumin

½ tsp chili powder

½ tsp garlic salt

½ tsp ground ginger

½ tsp ground cinnamon

Pinch of cayenne pepper

1 tbsp olive oil

1 cup/115 g raw unsalted pecans

1 cup/115 g raw unsalted almonds

Kosher salt

Preheat the oven to 325°F/165°C/gas 3.

In a small bowl, stir together all of the spices. Heat the olive oil in a small frying pan over medium heat. Add the spice mixture and cook, stirring constantly, until well blended and fragrant, about 3 minutes.

Combine the pecans and almonds in a large bowl. Add the spice mixture and toss well to coat evenly.

Spread the nuts in a single layer on a rimmed baking sheet/tray and toast in the oven, shaking the pan occasionally, until the nuts are lightly browned and the spices are fragrant, 12 to 15 minutes. Remove from the oven and sprinkle with salt while still warm. Let cool completely before serving.

**Make-Ahead:** The nuts will keep in an airtight container for up to 1 week. If they lose their crispness, reheat in an oven at 250°F/120°C/gas ½ for about 15 minutes, then let cool.

# deviled eggs niçoise

**makes 12 deviled eggs**

People are crazy for deviled eggs, among the most classic of picnic finger foods. Outdoors or in more elegant settings inside, whenever I serve them, they disappear quickly. This version springs from the hard-boiled eggs that are one of the definitive ingredients in *salade Niçoise*, and piles on other delicious flavors from that beloved French dish. These are wonderful with a chilled Muscadet or rosé.

6 large eggs
One 6-oz/170-g can water-
  or oil-packed tuna, drained
2 tbsp chopped Niçoise olives
1 tbsp capers, rinsed and drained
1 tbsp olive oil
2 tsp balsamic vinegar

1 tsp Dijon mustard
Freshly ground black pepper
12 small water- or salt-packed
  anchovy fillets (optional)
Finely chopped pimentos
  and red bell pepper/capsicum,
  peppadews, or green beans for garnish

Put the eggs in a large saucepan and add cold water to cover. Bring to a gentle boil over medium-high heat. When the water just begins to boil, remove the pot from the heat and cover tightly. Let the eggs stand, covered, for 30 minutes. Drain the eggs and rinse under cold running water. Pat the eggs dry and let cool completely.

When the eggs are cool enough to handle, peel them and cut in half lengthwise. Gently scoop the yolks into a large bowl, being careful not to break the whites. Arrange the egg white halves, cavity-side up, on a platter and set aside.

Add the tuna, olives, and capers to the bowl with the yolks and mix well with a fork, flaking the tuna finely and mashing the yolks until smooth. In a small bowl, whisk together the olive oil, vinegar, and mustard. Add the vinaigrette to the yolk mixture and stir to blend well. Season with pepper.

Using a small spoon, mound the filling in the cavities of the egg white halves, dividing it evenly. Top each with an anchovy fillet (if using) and garnish with the pimentos. Serve chilled or at room temperature.

*continued*

**Make-Ahead:** The deviled eggs can be made up to 3 hours in advance. Cover loosely with plastic wrap/cling film and refrigerate. Serve chilled or remove from the refrigerator 30 minutes before serving and serve at room temperature.

### Wine Bite Idea

Try these delicious filling variations for deviled eggs with fish, or create your own. Be sure to use good-quality mayo, or homemade (see page 116). To the egg yolks, add:

- ½ cup/120 ml mayonnaise, 1 tsp Dijon mustard, ¼ cup/40 g each finely chopped anchovies and celery, and freshly ground black pepper to taste.

- ½ cup/120 ml mayonnaise, 1 tsp Dijon mustard, ¼ cup/40 g finely chopped fresh lump crabmeat, and fresh lemon juice, salt, and freshly ground black pepper to taste.

- ½ cup/120 ml mayonnaise, 1 tsp Dijon mustard, ¼ cup/40 g finely chopped smoked salmon, 2 tbsp finely minced fresh dill, and fresh lemon juice to taste. Garnish each with a small dill sprig.

- ½ cup/120 ml mayonnaise, 1 tsp Dijon mustard, and fresh lemon juice, salt, and freshly ground black pepper to taste. Garnish each with a small cooked and chilled shrimp/prawn.

# marinated cerignola olives

**serves 10 to 12**

Big, beautiful Cerignolas are an olive lover's dream. Rich with a ripe olive flavor, they come in green, red, and black varieties; I like to sauté a colorful combination of all three with garlic and fresh herbs. They are delicious served warm or at room temperature, or spoon them into a jar with extra-virgin olive oil to cover and keep them on hand in the refrigerator. They're wonderful on their own or served with cheese and *salumi*. Serve with a Merlot or Sangiovese.

1 tbsp extra-virgin olive oil,
    plus ½ cup/120 ml
2 cloves garlic, thinly sliced
2 cups/500 g mixed Cerignola olives,
    rinsed and drained
6 pieces lemon peel,
    each about 1½ in/4 cm long
    and ½ in/12 mm wide

1 tsp chopped fresh rosemary
1 tsp chopped fresh thyme
Pinch of red pepper flakes (optional)
Freshly ground black pepper

Heat the 1 tbsp olive oil in a skillet over medium heat. Add the garlic and sauté until softened, about 2 minutes. Add the olives, lemon peel, rosemary, thyme, and red pepper flakes (if using). Season with black pepper. Cook gently, stirring occasionally, to allow the flavors to blend, about 10 minutes. Remove from the heat and let cool. Transfer the olives to a serving bowl.

Pour the ½ cup/120 ml olive oil over the olives and serve.

**Make-Ahead:** The olives will keep, tightly covered in the refrigerator, for up to 3 weeks.

# warm citrus & fennel olives

**serves 6 to 8**

When olives are warmed in a skillet with a bit of oil, they take on robust and meaty flavor. Add a squeeze of fresh orange juice and slivers of fresh fennel and their scent and taste are unforgettable. You may want to double or triple this recipe. The deep flavor of these olives goes very well with a full-bodied Cabernet Sauvignon.

1 cup/250 g mixed olives (see Note), rinsed and drained, 1 tbsp juice reserved

2 tbsp fresh orange juice

4 pieces orange peel, each about 1 in/2.5 cm long and ¼ in/6 mm wide

½ bulb fennel, trimmed, cored, and thinly sliced lengthwise

½ tsp fennel seed

½ tsp extra-virgin olive oil

Put the olives and reserved juice in a skillet. Add the orange juice, orange peel, fennel, fennel seed, and olive oil and place over medium-low heat. Cook, stirring occasionally, until the juices begin to simmer and then reduce slightly.

Transfer to a small serving bowl and serve warm, or remove from the heat, cover, and reheat the olives gently just before serving. Serve with toothpicks.

**Note:** There are dozens of varieties of olives that differ in size, color, and flavor. Use any combination of best-quality cured olives for this recipe. Following are a few suggestions for the mix. Be sure to have small bowls handy for olive pits.

- Cerignola (Italian): Large oval-shaped with a sweetish flavor. Red, green, or black in color.
- Gaeta (Italian): Black or brown, small, and wrinkled.
- Ligurian (Italian): Black or brown. The black ones are very flavorful.
- Niçoise (French): Very small and dark brown or black, with a large pit.
- Nyons (French): Small and known for their reddish-brown color.
- Picholine (French): Small and medium-green in color.
- Kalamata (Greek): Purple-black, almond shaped, and shiny. Available in a variety of sizes.

## Chapter 2

# DIPS & SPREADS

SUCCULENT TOPPINGS FOR
BREADS, CRACKERS, CHIPS & VEGETABLES

# bagna cauda

*Bagna cauda* (which translates as "hot bath") is a simple dish that originated in Piedmont, Italy. It is fun to serve for a small gathering because guests gather around a bowl of warm garlic-and-anchovy-scented oil and dip into it with vegetables such as cauliflower, fennel, carrots, and celery, along with crusty bread. Wines from the Piedmont region, such as Dolcetto d'Alba and Barolo, are excellent accompaniments. *Bagna cauda* also pairs very nicely with Pinot Noir.

6 to 8 olive oil–packed anchovy fillets

½ cup/120 ml extra-virgin olive oil

4 cloves garlic, finely minced

Red pepper flakes

½ cup/115 g unsalted butter

½ cup/60 g chopped fresh flat-leaf parsley

1 or 2 baguettes, cut into ½-in/12-mm slices

Bite-size pieces of raw cauliflower, fennel, carrot, celery, bell pepper/capsicum, and radish for serving

In a medium saucepan over high heat, combine the anchovies with 2 tbsp of the olive oil and heat until very hot, smashing the anchovies with the back of a wooden spoon until they have dissolved into the oil.

Add the garlic and red pepper flakes to taste and cook until the garlic is softened but not brown. Add the butter, the remaining olive oil, and the parsley and cook slowly over low heat until the butter is melted.

Place the saucepan of *bagna cauda* on a hot pad or warming tray on the serving table, or transfer to a fondue pot or chafing dish over a burner. Serve at once with the bread and vegetables.

# crabmeat dip

**serves 6 to 8**

This recipe is an old favorite from my family and is loosely based on a preparation for Crab Louis. It couldn't be more easy or delicious. Serve with crackers and fresh celery sticks. Chardonnay and Sauvignon Blanc always taste great with seafood; I think they especially complement the sweet and fresh ocean flavors of crabmeat.

½ cup/120 ml mayonnaise, homemade (see page 116) or good-quality commercial

2 tbsp bottled chili sauce

1 tbsp finely chopped red onion

1 tbsp chopped fresh flat-leaf parsley

1 tsp fresh lemon juice

Hot-pepper sauce

½ lb/225 g fresh lump crabmeat, picked over for cartilage and shell fragments

1 or 2 tbsp heavy (whipping)/double cream

Kosher salt and freshly ground black pepper

Crackers for serving

In a bowl, stir together the mayonnaise, chili sauce, onion, parsley, lemon juice, and a dash of hot-pepper sauce until well blended. Add the crabmeat and 1 tbsp cream and mix very gently. Be careful not to break up the crab too much. If the mixture seems too thin, gently stir in the remaining 1 tbsp cream. Season with salt and black pepper.

Refrigerate the dip until well chilled, at least 2 hours and up to 4 hours. Serve with the crackers and more hot sauce.

# fava bean dip

**serves 8 to 10**

Big, beautiful, fresh fava beans have a delicate nutty taste and their short season, which runs from late spring through summer, should be taken full advantage of and enjoyed. Try this wonderful dip with chips/ crisps and vegetables or spread it on crostini (see page 13). This dip, the Herbed White Bean Spread (page 34), and the Lentil & Goat Cheese Spread (page 35) are all very versatile in a wine setting and pair well with a range of whites from sparkling Prosecco to Burgundy. Good reds to drink with them include Pinot Noir, Merlot, and Côtes du Rhône.

2 lb/910 g fresh fava/broad beans, shelled (about 2 cups/280 g)

⅓ cup/75 ml olive oil

2 tbsp chopped fresh mint, plus whole leaves for garnish

1 clove garlic, peeled

1 tsp fresh lemon juice

2 tbsp ricotta cheese

1 tbsp freshly grated Parmesan cheese, plus more for garnish

Kosher salt and freshly ground black pepper

Rinse the shelled beans. Bring a large saucepan of lightly salted water to a boil over high heat. Reduce the heat to medium, add the beans, and cook until tender, 3 to 5 minutes. Drain in a colander and rinse under cold running water. Drain again thoroughly. Peel or pinch off the thin inner skins.

Combine the beans, olive oil, chopped mint, garlic, lemon juice, both cheeses, and salt and pepper to taste in a food processor and process until smooth. Taste and adjust the seasoning, and process again just until combined.

Transfer the bean dip to a small serving bowl. Garnish with additional Parmesan cheese and the mint leaves and serve at once.

**Make-Ahead:** The bean dip will keep, tightly covered in the refrigerator, for up to 2 days. Bring to room temperature and garnish before serving.

# herbed white bean spread

**serves 4 to 6**

This fantastic spread is good to serve on its own with grilled bread, or you may want to add an array of toppings. As with other bean dips, the wines here can vary from subtle, to enjoy the light earthy essence of the beans, as with a sparkling white, to bold, for example a medium-bodied Merlot to mingle with the herbs and citrus.

2 tbsp olive oil

1 small red onion, coarsely chopped

4 cloves garlic, cut in half lengthwise

One 15½-oz/445-g can cannellini beans, rinsed and drained

2 tbsp chopped fresh flat-leaf parsley

1 tsp chopped fresh chives

1 tsp chopped fresh thyme

Kosher salt and freshly ground black pepper

1 tbsp crème fraîche

1 tbsp fresh lemon juice, or to taste

Basic Bruschetta (page 76), crostini (see page 13), or crackers for serving

Roasted red or yellow bell pepper/capsicum strips, pimientos, seeded and chopped *piquillo* peppers, chopped black or green olives, anchovy fillets, caramelized onions, or capers, or a combination for garnish

Heat the olive oil in a large sauté pan over medium heat. Add the onion and garlic and cook, stirring often, until softened and lightly golden, about 5 minutes. Add the beans, parsley, chives, thyme, and salt and pepper to taste and cook, stirring occasionally, until the beans are heated through and the flavors have blended, about 10 minutes. Remove from the heat and let cool slightly.

When the bean mixture is cool enough to handle, transfer to a food processor. Add the crème fraîche and lemon juice and process until smooth. Taste and adjust the seasoning with salt, pepper, and lemon juice, if necessary. Process again if needed just to combine.

Serve at once with the grilled bread and garnishes of your choice alongside.

**Make-Ahead:** The bean spread will keep, tightly covered in the refrigerator, for up to 3 days. Bring to room temperature and garnish before serving.

# lentil & goat cheese spread

**serves 8 to 10**

This spread has a nice, nutty flavor that goes well with lightly salted pita or bagel chips, crackers, or Parmesan toasts. A wide range of wines complements this mélange of savory and sour—try a white Burgundy or your favorite Côtes du Rhône.

1 cup/200 g brown or green lentils

1 small yellow onion, peeled

1 clove garlic, peeled

1 carrot, peeled

1 stalk celery, trimmed

6 fresh flat-leaf parsley sprigs, ½ cup/15 g chopped fresh flat-leaf parsley, plus more for garnish

2 cups/480 ml chicken stock or low-sodium broth

4 oz/115 g goat cheese, softened and crumbled

2 tsp fresh lemon juice

1 tsp celery salt

Pinch of cayenne pepper

Kosher salt and freshly ground black pepper

Extra-virgin olive oil for drizzling

Pita or bagel chips, crackers, or Parmesan Toasts (page 80) for serving

Place the lentils in a colander, rinse thoroughly, and drain.

In a soup pot, combine the lentils, onion, garlic, carrot, celery, parsley sprigs, stock, and ½ cup/ 120 ml water. Bring to a boil over medium-high heat, then reduce the heat to medium-low and simmer gently until the lentils are very tender, about 30 minutes. Drain the lentils and let cool. Discard the onion, garlic, carrot, celery, and parsley sprigs.

Transfer the lentils to a food processor. Add the goat cheese, chopped parsley, lemon juice, celery salt, cayenne pepper, and salt and black pepper to taste and process until very smooth. Taste and adjust the seasoning, if necessary. Process again if needed just to combine.

Transfer to a small serving bowl. Drizzle with olive oil, garnish with a little more chopped parsley, and serve at once with the chips, crackers, or toasts.

# smoked salmon & caper spread

**serves 6 to 8**

Smoked salmon is always an elegant treat. Here it is made into a lip-smacking spread that's lovely on pumpernickel bread or baguettes, and even more terrific topped with fresh tomatoes and red onion slices. White wine is famously fabulous with fish, and here some bubbles are a pleasant foil to the rich cream cheese. Serve with Champagne, sparkling wine, or Cava.

One 8-oz/225-g package cream cheese, at room temperature

1 tbsp milk

¼ cup/10 g chopped fresh flat-leaf parsley

2 tbsp fresh lemon juice

1 tsp capers, rinsed and drained

Dash of hot-pepper sauce

4 oz/115 g smoked salmon, coarsely chopped

Freshly ground black pepper

Toasted pumpernickel bread or baguette slices, chopped or sliced fresh tomatoes, and thinly sliced red onion for serving

Combine the cream cheese, milk, parsley, lemon juice, capers, hot-pepper sauce, and about three-fourths of the salmon in a food processor and process until smooth. Add the remaining salmon, season with black pepper, and pulse until just incorporated.

Spread on the toasted bread, top with the tomatoes and slivers of onion, and serve at once.

**Make-Ahead:** The salmon spread will keep, covered, in the refrigerator for up to 2 days. Bring to room temperature before serving.

**Wine Bite Idea**

For a quick and easy brunch buffet, arrange the salmon spread, tomatoes, and red onions on a platter with warm toasted bagels for guests to assemble themselves. Complete the menu with a Swiss Chard, Mushroom & Chorizo Frittata (page 72), green salad, and Fresh Fruit with Mascarpone Cheese (page 146).

# creamy chicken liver & date spread

**serves 6 to 8**

I first tasted this silky-smooth spread at The New French, a lively bistro in Manhattan's West Village. The chef, Livio Velardo, was kind enough to give me the recipe. It's wonderful for the holidays! Serve this creamy spread on warm, crusty bread or pumpernickel toasts with any full-bodied red wine.

1¼ lb/570 g chicken livers

2 cups/480 ml whole milk

6 shallots, peeled

4 cloves garlic, peeled

3 tbsp canola oil

Kosher salt
   and freshly ground black pepper

½ cup/115 g unsalted butter,
   at room temperature

4 Medjool dates, pitted and chopped

2 tbsp sherry vinegar

Warmed crusty bread or pumpernickel toasts
   for serving

Drain the chicken livers, rinse well, and pat dry on paper towels/absorbent paper. Remove any connective tissue. Place the chicken livers in a bowl, pour the milk over, and let soak overnight, covered, in the refrigerator.

Preheat the oven to 375°F/190°C/gas 5. Put the shallots and garlic in a medium roasting pan/tray, drizzle with 1 tbsp of the canola oil, and toss to coat. Roast until soft and golden, about 20 minutes. Remove from the oven and set aside.

Drain and rinse the chicken livers again and pat dry on paper towels/absorbent paper. Season with salt and pepper. In a large skillet over medium-high heat, melt 1 tbsp of the butter in the remaining 2 tbsp canola oil. Add the chicken livers, a few at a time if necessary to avoid crowding the pan, and cook, turning occasionally, until lightly browned and firm but still slightly pink in the center, 4 to 5 minutes. Do not overcook. Transfer to the roasting pan and toss together with the garlic and shallots. Add the dates to the pan. Drizzle everything with the vinegar and toss again to coat.

Transfer half of the chicken liver mixture to a blender or food processor and add half of the remaining butter. Process until smooth. Taste and adjust the seasoning, then transfer to a serving bowl. Repeat with the remaining liver mixture and butter. Cover and refrigerate until well chilled and firm, at least 4 hours or up to overnight. Spread on the bread or crostini and serve at once, or pass the spread and bread separately.

Chapter 3

# CHEESE

Creamy, Good Cheese Dishes
That Pair Perfectly with Wine

# cheese fondue

**serves 6 to 8**

Fondue is a lot of fun to serve to a crowd for an informal get-together. Serve it warm in a fondue pot or a heavy saucepan with lots of bread and vegetables for delicious dipping. There is no consensus on which wine to drink with fondue, probably because it's virtually universally compatible. Some think it's best to drink the white wine that the fondue was made with, while others prefer a dry red. My personal choice would be a Gewürztraminer. Eat, sip, and enjoy.

1 clove garlic, cut in half crosswise

1 cup/240 ml dry white wine

½ lb/225 g Swiss cheese, shredded (about 2 cups)

½ lb/225 g Gruyère cheese, shredded (about 2 cups)

1 tbsp cornstarch/cornflour

1 tbsp cherry brandy such as kirsch

1 tbsp fresh lemon juice

½ tsp dry mustard

Pinch of freshly grated nutmeg

Accompaniments of your choice, such as cubes of bread, roasted fingerling potatoes, blanched asparagus, broccoli and cauliflower florets, bell pepper/capsicum strips, and/or carrot sticks

Rub the inside of a large heavy soup pot with the cut sides of the garlic, then discard the garlic. Add the wine to the pot and bring to a low simmer over medium heat.

Gradually add the cheeses to the pot and cook, stirring constantly, until they are just melted and creamy; do not let boil.

In a small bowl, whisk together the cornstarch/cornflour, brandy, lemon juice, mustard, and nutmeg until well blended and stir into the fondue. Bring the fondue to a simmer and cook, stirring, until thickened, 5 to 8 minutes.

Transfer to a fondue pot set over a flame or serve directly from the soup pot. Arrange the bread and vegetables on a platter and serve with fondue forks or skewers.

# stilton-stuffed dates with prosciutto

**makes 12 stuffed and wrapped dates; serves 6**

Warm dates stuffed with cheese and wrapped with bacon/streaky bacon or prosciutto are a wildly popular tapa, or bar snack—and with good reason. The combination of sweet, savory, and salty flavors is irresistible. There are many variations of this dish to try; my personal favorite is made with Stilton cheese and prosciutto. See the Wine Bite Idea, below, for other palate-pleasing date-and-cheese combinations. Savor with a glass of Pinot Grigio or Chianti.

12 Medjool dates, pitted
2 to 3 oz/55 to 85 g Stilton cheese, crumbled
6 thin slices prosciutto, cut in half lengthwise

Preheat the oven to 350°F/180°C/gas 4. Line a baking sheet/tray with aluminum foil.

Cut a lengthwise slit in each date. Stuff each one with just enough of the cheese to fill the cavity but not spill out. Pinch the stuffed dates closed.

Wrap each date in a piece of prosciutto and arrange them, seam-side down, on the prepared pan.

Bake for 10 minutes. Remove from the oven and, using tongs, carefully turn the dates. Return to the oven and bake until browned and crisp, about 10 minutes longer. Serve warm or at room temperature.

**Make-Ahead:** The dates can be prepared up to 3 hours ahead of time before baking. Cover and refrigerate until ready to bake.

### Wine Bite Idea
The dates can be stuffed with myriad cheeses from sharp to sweet: try blues such as Maytag or Gorgonzola, tangy goat cheese or fresh mozzarella, sweetish mascarpone and domestic cream cheeses, or the classic salty bite of Parmesan. In place of the prosciutto, wrap in bacon strips or thin slices of Serrano or Parma ham.

# cheddar cheese crisps

**makes about 3 dozen 2-in/5-cm crisps; serves 6 to 8**

The key to making these delicious crisps is to chill the dough fully before cutting it into thin rounds. They are great when you're planning your prep time for a party, because the dough must be made in advance. The light but rich, cheesy crisps are perfect washed down with a glass of sparkling wine.

1 cup/130 g unbleached all-purpose/plain flour

1 cup/115 g freshly shredded sharp Cheddar cheese

4 tbsp/55 g unsalted butter, at room temperature

Pinch of cayenne pepper

Kosher salt

¼ cup/35 g sesame seeds, lightly toasted (see Note)

In a food processor, combine the flour, cheese, butter, cayenne, and salt to taste and process until smooth. Scrape the dough onto a lightly floured work surface and roll into a rope about 1½ in/4 cm in diameter. Wrap in plastic wrap/cling film, and refrigerate for 30 minutes to allow the dough to firm slightly.

Remove the dough from the refrigerator and unwrap it; it will still be soft, but should be easy to shape now. On a clean, lightly floured work surface, roll the dough into a log about 2 in/5 cm in diameter and 8 in/20 cm long. Wrap the log in clean plastic wrap/cling film. If baking the crisps the same day, put the dough in the freezer until firm and well chilled, about 1 hour, then transfer to the refrigerator until you are ready to bake.

Preheat the oven to 350°F/180°C/gas 4. Unwrap the log and cut into slices about ¼ inch/6 mm thick. Arrange the slices on baking sheets/trays about 1 in/2.5 cm apart, sprinkle the tops with the sesame seeds, and bake until lightly browned, about 10 minutes. Using a spatula, transfer the crisps to a wire rack and let cool for a few minutes. Serve warm or at room temperature.

**Note:** To toast sesame seeds, place them in a small dry frying pan over medium-low heat and cook, stirring constantly, until fragrant and lightly toasted, 2 to 3 minutes; the seeds can burn quickly. Immediately pour onto a plate to cool.

**Make-Ahead:** The dough can be made in advance and kept, wrapped tightly in the refrigerator, for up to 2 days. You can also freeze the dough for later use; wrap tightly and use within 1 week. Bring to refrigerator temperature a day before baking.

# gougères

**makes about 3 dozen hors d'oeuvres; serves 6 to 8**

Gougères, the classic elegant cheese puffs from France, are little bites of cheesy choux pastry—crisp on the outside, airy on the inside—perfect for serving with wine, especially red. Traditionally gougères are made exclusively with Gruyère cheese, but they're quite wonderful with a combination of cheeses like the Swiss, Cheddar, and Parmesan in this recipe. The puffs really taste best when served warm from the oven, but they may be made ahead of time and reheated, if necessary. These bite-size beauties go well with French Pinot Noir or Côtes du Rhône.

4 tbsp/55 g unsalted butter
½ tsp kosher salt
1½ cups/190 g unbleached all-purpose/
   plain flour
3 large eggs
½ cup/60 g freshly shredded Swiss-style cheese
   such as Gruyère, Comté, or Emmenthal

½ cup/60 g freshly shredded
   sharp Cheddar cheese
½ cup/60 g freshly grated Parmesan cheese
Freshly ground black pepper

Preheat the oven to 425°F/220°C/gas 7. Lightly grease two baking sheets/trays.

In a medium saucepan, combine the butter, salt, and 1 cup/240 ml water. Slowly bring to a boil over medium-high heat. Cook, stirring, until the butter melts. Add the flour all at once and cook, stirring constantly, until the dough holds together in a ball, about 5 minutes. The dough will get stiffer as you stir; continue stirring until the dough is smooth. Transfer to a large bowl or the bowl of a stand mixer.

Using an electric mixer set on high speed, add the eggs one at a time, beating well after each addition. Stop beating when the mixture is glossy. Stir in the cheeses and season with pepper.

Drop by teaspoonfuls onto the prepared sheets/trays and bake until lightly browned and puffed, about 12 minutes. Serve hot, warm, or at room temperature.

### Wine Bite Idea

Gougères can be made with a variety of other cheeses, such as fontina, taleggio, or blue, or a combination. And after you stir the cheese(s) into the dough, you can add other ingredients such as finely chopped crisp-cooked bacon, minced fresh chives or arugula, and/or spices like sweet paprika, freshly grated nutmeg, cayenne pepper, and chili powder.

# pita & feta cheese nachos

**serves 8 to 10**

Homemade pita chips are very easy to make and taste much better than store-bought. This is a nice light wine snack to serve in summer with peak-of-season ripe tomatoes and cucumbers. This versatile dish goes wonderfully with a dry rosé.

Eight 6- or 8-in/15- or 20-cm pita pockets,
 cut into wedges
¾ cup/180 ml olive oil, plus more
 for drizzling (optional)
1 tsp paprika
Kosher salt
2 cups/280 g crumbled feta cheese
1 cup/240 ml Greek yogurt,
 preferably whole-milk

½ cup/15 g chopped fresh mint, plus more for garnish
1 tsp fresh lemon juice
Freshly ground black pepper
1 red onion, chopped
3 fresh ripe tomatoes, chopped
1 cucumber, peeled and chopped
½ cup/115 g Kalamata olives, pitted and halved

Preheat the oven to 350°F/180°C/gas 4.

Arrange the pita wedges in a single layer on baking sheets/trays. In a small bowl, whisk together the ¾ cup/180 ml olive oil and paprika. Using a pastry brush, brush the pita wedges with the seasoned oil. Sprinkle with salt. Bake the chips, turning once, just until they begin to turn brown, about 10 minutes. Turn off the oven and keep the chips warm in it.

In a food processor, combine the feta, yogurt, ½ cup/15 g mint, and lemon juice. Season with pepper. Process until smooth. Taste and adjust the seasoning, if necessary.

In a large bowl, combine the onion, tomatoes, cucumber, and olives and toss to mix well. Put the chips on a large serving plate and top with the feta cheese mixture and the tomato mixture. Drizzle with a bit of olive oil, if desired, garnish with mint, and serve at once.

# manchego quesadillas with roasted red peppers & onions

**makes 16 wedges; serves 6 to 8**

Wedges of tortilla, filled with roasted vegetables and oozing with warm melted Manchego cheese—the sheep's-milk variety that is a specialty of Spain; with a firm texture, distinctive, subtle piquancy; and very pleasing melting quality—make a surprisingly elegant snack. Try these quesadillas with a Spanish wine like a red Rioja or white Albariño.

2 red bell peppers/capsicums,
seeded and quartered
2 red onions, peeled and quartered
1 to 2 tbsp olive oil
Kosher salt and freshly ground black pepper

Corn or canola oil for frying
Eight 6- or 8-in/15- or 20-cm flour tortillas
2 cups/240 g grated Manchego cheese

Preheat the oven to 350°F/180°C/gas 4.

Put the bell peppers/capsicums and onions on a baking sheet/tray. Drizzle with the olive oil and toss to coat. Sprinkle with salt and pepper. Roast, turning once, until browned and softened on all sides, about 1 hour. Remove from the oven and set aside to cool. Chop the roasted vegetables into small dice, then transfer to a bowl and toss to mix.

Heat a sauté pan over high heat. Reduce the heat to medium and add just enough of the corn oil to coat the bottom of the pan, swirling the pan or spreading the oil with a spatula. Let the oil heat briefly, then place a tortilla in the pan and sprinkle with ¼ cup/30 g of the cheese. Add one-fourth of the vegetable mixture, top with another ¼ cup cheese, and cover with a second tortilla. Cover and cook until golden brown on the bottom, about 3 minutes. Turn carefully and cook until the cheese is melted and the second tortilla is golden brown, about 3 minutes longer. Repeat with the remaining tortillas, cheese, and vegetable mixture to make three more quesadillas. Let cool before cutting. Cut each into quarters and serve.

**Make-Ahead:** The roasted peppers and onions can be made up to 1 day in advance. Store, covered tightly, in the refrigerator. Gently reheat the vegetable mixture in a sauté pan over low heat before assembling the quesadillas.

# spinach, swiss chard & feta cheese pie

**serves 10 to 12**

The combination of spinach and Swiss chard is a tasty twist on Greek spanakopita. This "pie" has no crust, held together instead by cooked greens and a rich, moist egg filling, so it's very easy to cut into any size squares or wedges you like. This dish is great light, warm-weather fare, and goes well with almost any chilled white wine or rosé.

2 tbsp olive oil

2 lb/910 g fresh spinach, rinsed and stemmed

1 lb/455 g Swiss chard, rinsed and stemmed

6 large eggs

1 cup/115 g crumbled feta cheese

¾ cup/90 g freshly grated Parmesan cheese

Freshly ground black pepper

2 tbsp pine nuts or chopped walnut

Preheat the oven to 375°F/190°C/gas 5. Coat a 2-qt/2-L baking dish with 1 tbsp of the olive oil.

Fill a large pot with water and bring to a boil. Add the spinach and Swiss chard and cook until wilted, about 1 minute. Drain and let cool. Squeeze out as much liquid as possible and coarsely chop.

In a large bowl, whisk the eggs with the feta, ½ cup/60 g of the Parmesan, and pepper to taste. Stir in the spinach, chard, and pine nuts and mix thoroughly. Spoon the mixture into the baking dish and smooth out. Sprinkle the remaining ¼ cup/30 g of Parmesan cheese on top. Drizzle the remaining olive oil over the pie and bake until golden and sizzling, 35 to 40 minutes. Let cool for about 5 minutes, then cut into small serving-size squares or wedges, bite-size cubes, or another shape as you like, and serve.

**Make-Ahead:** The pie can be baked and refrigerated up to 1 day ahead of time. Bring to room temperature before reheating.

# caramelized onion & cheese squares

**makes about 3 dozen squares; serves 6 to 8**

These elegant squares are made with slow-cooked caramelized onions, pungent blue cheese, and tangy goat cheese. They're a terrific addition to the holiday buffet table or to serve as an hors d'oeuvre before dinner or at a cocktail party. Cabernets pair very nicely with blue cheese dishes.

**Crust:**

2 cups/255 g unbleached all-purpose/ plain flour

2 tsp baking powder

½ tsp kosher salt

¾ cup/180 ml whole milk

¼ cup/60 ml olive oil

2 tbsp unsalted butter, melted

**Topping:**

2 tbsp unsalted butter

2 tbsp olive oil

3 large red onions (about 2 lb/910 g), thinly sliced

1 tbsp finely chopped fresh thyme

1 tsp sugar

Kosher salt and freshly ground black pepper

½ cup/70 g crumbled blue cheese

½ cup/70 g crumbled fresh goat cheese

Preheat the oven to 425°F/220°C/gas 7.

To make the crust: In a medium bowl, stir together the flour, baking powder, and salt. Make a well in the center of the mixture. In a measuring cup, whisk together the milk, olive oil, and melted butter. Slowly pour the milk mixture into the well, stirring until just blended and the mixture comes together into a rough mass. Turn out the dough onto a lightly floured work surface and roll out into a 10-by-13-in/25-by-33-cm rectangle. Transfer the dough to a baking sheet/tray. Pierce the dough all over with a fork.

To make the topping: In a large skillet over medium heat, melt the butter with the olive oil. Add the onions and cook, stirring frequently, until softened and lightly browned, about 10 minutes. Add the thyme, sugar, and salt and pepper to taste, reduce the heat to low, and cook, stirring frequently, until the onions are soft and caramelized, about 20 minutes.

Spread the onion mixture evenly over the dough. Sprinkle with the cheeses, cut into squares with a pizza wheel or a sharp knife, and bake until the crust is golden and the cheese is bubbling, about 20 minutes. Transfer to a wire rack and let cool a bit on the pan. Serve warm or at room temperature.

# wine & cheese

A wine-and-cheese party is a casually elegant style of gathering that's just right for any occasion. A platter of sumptuous cheeses served with fresh fruit, crusty bread, and other accompaniments is always enticing, but choosing from the many types of cheese on the market today can be staggering. This section will provide a useful guide to different styles of cheese and their origins, as well as serving recommendations.

The choice of wines to serve with cheese is wide and varied—from light and simple whites to rich, dense reds—and the fun part of this informal get-together is discovering new pairings while sipping and tasting a variety of wines and cheeses.

## the cheese board

For exceptional color and taste, serve a selection of fresh fruits, such as apples, pears, plums, figs, and grapes, and dried fruits, such as apricots and raisins, with the cheese. And don't forget to add other accompaniments to the platter like wild honey, fig jam and cherry preserves, and walnuts, almonds, and pistachios.

There are no hard and fast rules about serving cheese, but a good rule of thumb is to serve three to six different cheeses that vary in size, shape, texture, and color and that run from soft to semi-soft to hard. When making your selection, look for cheeses with contrasting flavors from mild to strong and choose ones from the cow, sheep, and goat milk families. For a cocktail or cheese-tasting party, think in terms of serving 5 to 6 oz/140 to 170 g per person. Be sure to serve cheese at room temperature—*never* cold. Cut just before serving to avoid drying out.

There are many different categories of cheese, and it's a nice idea to choose a few cheeses from each one. Following is a sampling.

## hard cheeses

Hard cheeses are often only thought of as "grating cheese." But many hard cheeses are packed with flavor and deserve a place on any great cheese plate.

**Asiago:** This cheese is made from part-skim cow's milk. It has a rich, nutty flavor and is good with peasant bread and black olives.

**Dry Jack:** This is a Monterey Jack cheese that is aged 6 months to 2 years. It is reminiscent of Parmesan but is less grainy. It is very good with ripe apples, plums, and figs.

**Parmigiano-Reggiano:** The king of Italian grating cheeses has a wonderful, rich nutty flavor and is well worth its premium price. Although it is best known as the cheese to be sprinkled or shaved over pasta, it is also a superb dessert cheese. It is especially good with ripe pears and walnuts.

*Hard cheeses, typically also sharp, pair well with Cabernet Sauvignon and Merlot wines.*

## semifirm cheeses

The range of cheeses in this category is wide—from aged sheep's milk to Cheddar to Swiss-style cheeses. They're all quite wonderful and should be well represented on the cheese platter.

**Aged sheep's-milk cheese:** There is a variety of these cheeses from all over the world to choose from. Among them are Prince de Claverolle and Etorki, from France's Western Pyrénées; Brin d'Amour, from Corsica; *pecorino toscano*, the sheep's-milk cheeses made in Tuscany; and Manchego, from the Castilla-La Mancha region in Spain. These cheeses have a piquant and nutty flavor.

**Cheddar:** Cheddars are best when aged at least 6 months; of those, there is a wide variety to choose from. Well-known English Cheddars include Double Gloucester, Lancashire, and salty crumbly Wensleydale. Among notable Cheddars from other areas of the world are Black Diamond Cheddar, from Canada; Grafton Village from Vermont; and Tillamook Cheddar, from Oregon. Cheddar cheese is delicious with apples and grapes.

**Emmenthaler:** The original Swiss cheese has a distinctly nutty flavor. It is very good with plums.

**Gruyère:** This heartier, nuttier Swiss is best known for its use in fondues, quiches, and tarts. But it is also very good when served on its own or with thinly sliced sausage or salami. Comté, a French Gruyère, is a bit firmer and drier than the Swiss version. It is an excellent base for quiches and tarts as well as fondue. It also goes very well with mild-flavored sausages.

*These cheeses pair well with Chardonnay, Pinot Noir, and Syrah wines.*

## blue cheeses

Blue cheeses range from soft, creamy, and mild to intense and firm. They pair beautifully with a variety of wines. Here are a few examples of excellent blue cheeses.

**Blue de Bresse:** A creamy, mild blue cheese from France. It is lovely to serve with fresh figs.

**Gorgonzola:** This rich and pungent cheese from Italy is a star in salads (famously with crunchy Belgian endive/chicory and toasted walnuts or pecans) and also a very good addition to a dessert cheese plate alongside ripe apples, pears, and walnuts.

**Maytag blue:** This tangy blue from Maytag Dairy Farms in Iowa is delicious served with poached pears and roasted figs.

**Roquefort:** This pungent, aged sheep's-milk blue cheese is, just as it sounds, from France. It has a soft, creamy texture and goes beautifully with figs and nuts.

**Stilton:** This assertive blue-mold cheese is from England. It has a very rich flavor and aftertaste. It is excellent with grapes.

*Blue cheeses pair well with Cabernet Sauvignon, Cabernet Franc, Zinfandel, and Sauternes wines.*

## semisoft cheeses

The smooth and buttery flavors and soft textures of these semisoft cheeses make them perennial party favorites to serve with a variety of wines.

**Fontina:** This creamy cow's-milk cheese has a mild, nutty flavor. Although it is best known as an Italian cheese, fontina is also made in Denmark, France, and the United States.

**Gouda and Edam :** These all-purpose cheeses from Holland go well with apples and pears.

**Morbier:** This aromatic cow's-milk cheese from France is defined by the dark vein of vegetable ash that streaks through its center. It has a nutty taste.

**Muenster:** The flavor of French Muenster cheese ranges from mild to assertive. This nuanced and refined style of Muenster cheese bears no resemblance to bland supermarket Muenster cheeses.

**Port Salut:** This cow's-milk cheese has a mild, creamy flavor and a very smooth texture.

**Reblechon:** When perfectly ripe, this French cow's-milk cheese has a mild and delicate flavor and should be eaten immediately. Because it continues to ripen after refrigeration, it can become bitter when it stands too long.

**Taleggio:** The flavor of this rich cheese from the Lombardy region of Italy can range from mild to pungent as it ages. It is very good with fresh peaches, plums, and cherries.

*These cheeses pair well with Riesling and Pinot Gris wines.*

## soft-ripened cheeses

These cheeses are big crowd-pleasers and good choices for parties. Look for cheese with a clean white rind—if the rind has lines, dark spots, or a brownish tinge, the cheese may be overripe and no longer desirable. Try to buy a whole wheel of cheese rather than a cut wedge.

**Brie:** Brie is probably the most popular French cheese in the United States. It has a smooth and buttery flavor. To check for ripeness, the cheese should be supple, not stiff to the touch. Brie is delicious when served with crisp baguettes and juicy ripe peaches, pears, and grapes.

**Camembert:** This is a wonderful rich and creamy cheese. Good, buttery Camemberts include the popular Valée and Le Chatelaine brands from France and the superb Blythedale Farms from Vermont. Be careful not to cut Camembert before it is fully ripened or it will never achieve its full potential.

*These cheeses pair well with Chardonnay, Pinot Blanc, and Pinot Noir wines.*

## double and triple crème cheeses

These rich and luscious cow's-milk cheeses are enriched with cream. Double crème cheeses contain a minimum of 60 percent butterfat and triple crèmes must have at least 75 percent. These soft and subtly sweet cheeses are delicate, so it is best to buy them whole instead of in cuts.

**L'Explorateur:** This delicious triple crème has a delightfully smooth flavor and a rich, buttery texture.

**Saint André:** This creamy, buttery triple crème has a mildly sweet finish.

*These cheeses pair well with Chardonnay and Merlot wines.*

## chèvres

Goat cheese, also known as chèvre, has a distinctive tart and tangy flavor. Although some of the better-known chèvres, such as Boucheron and Montrachet, are produced in France, there are many wonderful farmstead goat cheeses being produced domestically.

These tangy goat's-milk cheeses are very good with olives, capers, and fruity olive oil. They are also delicious served with figs, berries, and grapes for dessert.

**Boucheron:** These white, log-shaped chèvres have a smooth, buttery texture and medium-tart flavor.

**Crottin:** These button-shaped goat cheeses are lovely to serve drizzled with olive oil, fresh herbs, and freshly ground black pepper.

**Montrachet:** This well-known white chèvre from Burgundy has a soft, creamy texture. It is excellent with figs and nuts.

**Fresh chèvres:** Although these luscious fresh cheeses used to be rare in America, small farms from regions all over the country are producing excellent handcrafted fresh goat cheeses. A few good ones to look for are Laura Chenel, from California; Coach Farms, from New York; and Consider Bardwell, from Vermont.

*These cheeses pair well with Rosé, Pinot Gris, and Sauvignon Blanc wines.*

*Chapter 4*

# PIZZAS, TARTS & FRITTATAS

HEAVENLY HOMEMADE BITES
FRESH FROM THE OVEN

# basic pizza dough

**makes enough for two 12-in/30.5-cm pizzas**

Everybody loves homemade pizza! What's better than a scrumptious homemade pie right out of the oven? It's perfect party food because it can be as simple or as elaborate as you wish, using a classic-combo tomato sauce with fresh basil and a scattering of cheese or a mélange of fabulous ingredients. Dough and sauce can be made from scratch, or you can buy premade dough and good-quality tomato sauce/puree from a well-stocked supermarket or your local gourmet or Italian-foods market or pizzeria. I recommend investing in a pizza stone and paddle; they make a big difference in the authenticity of the crust and overall quality of the pizza. But in a pinch, sturdy baking sheets/trays will do.

1 cup/240 ml warm water

1 package active dry yeast

3 tbsp olive oil, plus more for brushing

Kosher salt

3 cups/385 g unbleached all-purpose/plain flour,
  plus more for dusting

Pour the warm water into a large bowl. Sprinkle the yeast over it and let stand until the yeast dissolves and gets a little foamy, about 5 minutes. Whisk in the 3 tbsp olive oil and a pinch of salt. Using a wooden spoon, beat in the flour, ½ cup/65 g at a time, until a soft and sticky dough forms; you may not need all of the flour. Turn the dough out onto a lightly floured work surface and knead until smooth, 8 to 10 minutes. Dust with flour as needed to prevent sticking.

Brush another large bowl with olive oil. Divide the dough into two balls and transfer to the bowl. Cover with a clean kitchen towel and let rise in a warm place until doubled in bulk, about 2½ hours.

If using the dough right away, gently separate the balls of dough (if needed) and place on a lightly dusted work surface. When you flatten the balls, gently press out the air but do not pack the dough. Proceed with the recipe as directed.

If not using the dough right away, store in the refrigerator for up to 1 day. Bring to room temperature before rolling out. Or, wrap the dough tightly and freeze for up to 1 month. Thaw in the refrigerator before using, about 3 hours. Bring to room temperature before rolling out.

# pizza with caramelized red onions, gorgonzola & sausage

**makes two 12-in/30.5-cm pizzas**

Here's a fantastic pizza combo to serve straight from the oven to your wine-sipping friends hanging around in the kitchen. Whenever you're making homemade pizza, be sure to have all of the ingredients prepped and ready to go. Although many American pizza lovers think that the only thing to drink with pizza is beer, hearty reds in the Italian tradition, like Chianti and Valpolicella, taste great with the hot, cheesy pies.

2 tbsp olive oil

1 tbsp unsalted butter

4 medium red onions, thinly sliced

Kosher salt
  and freshly ground black pepper

½ lb/225 g ground sausage
  such as pork, chicken, or turkey

1 recipe Basic Pizza Dough (facing page)

Cornmeal for dusting

1½ lb/225 g Gorgonzola cheese,
  crumbled (about 2 cups)

Freshly grated Parmesan cheese for garnish

In a large skillet over medium heat, melt the butter in the olive oil. Add the onions, season with salt and pepper, reduce the heat to medium-low, and cook slowly, stirring occasionally, until the onions are nicely browned and caramelized, about 30 minutes. Remove from the heat and set aside.

In a medium skillet over medium heat, cook the sausage, using a wooden spoon to break up the meat, until lightly browned, about 5 minutes. Using a slotted spoon, transfer the sausage to paper towels/absorbent paper to drain.

Preheat the oven to 450°F/230°C/gas 8 and put a pizza stone or heavy-bottomed baking sheet/tray in it to heat.

*continued*

To assemble the pizzas, flatten the first ball of dough on a surface dusted with cornmeal. Using a rolling pin, roll out the dough into a circle to roughly 12 in/30 cm in diameter and about ¼ in/ 6 mm thick. Dust a pizza paddle or baking sheet/tray with cornmeal and transfer the pizza dough onto it. Working very quickly, spoon half of the onions and sausage over the dough round, spreading them with the back of the spoon to cover and leaving a ½-in/12-mm border. Sprinkle with half of the Gorgonzola. Garnish the pizza with Parmesan and additional freshly ground black pepper. Slide the pizza from the paddle directly into the oven onto the pizza stone or baking sheet/tray and bake until the dough is golden brown and the cheeses are bubbly and golden, about 15 minutes. Cut the pizza into narrow wedges and serve at once. Repeat to make the second pizza.

## using store-bought pizza dough

*If you don't have time to make pizza dough from scratch, a good alternative is to purchase prepared dough from the supermarket. Pizza dough is remarkably forgiving when it comes to storing and traveling, and good-quality commercial versions, usually found in the dairy section in supermarkets, bake up impressively close to homemade dough in texture and taste. Other good sources include specialty Italian markets, cheese stores, or your favorite pizza place. It's a kind of magical thing to have on hand in your refrigerator or freezer, making for an instantly festive and, with the addition of just a few seasonal ingredients, beautiful meal or hors d'oeuvre.*

### Other tips for using purchased dough:

- Allow refrigerated dough to come to room temperature before working with it.

- Roll the dough out as thinly as possible before adding toppings.

- If you're not using the dough right away (and it hasn't already been frozen), freeze it, wrapped tightly in plastic wrap/cling film, within 2 days of buying it. It will last for up to 1 month. Thaw in the refrigerator, about 3 hours. Bring to room temperature before rolling out.

# pizza with shallots, mixed greens & fontina cheese

**makes two 12-in/30.5-cm pizzas**

In pizza making, there are no hard and fast rules to follow; it is perhaps one of the most free-form culinary arts. In this recipe, you can use almost any type of cooking green, depending on what you like and what's in season. The same goes for the cheese—almost any semisoft cheese will work well. And if you don't have time to make homemade dough, you can make this delicious pizza with any good commercial dough (see facing page). Try this with Chianti or Rioja.

3 tbsp olive oil

4 large shallots, finely chopped

2 lb/910 g Swiss chard, rinsed

1½ lb/680 g mixed greens such as dandelion greens, kale, or spinach, rinsed and stemmed

Red pepper flakes (optional)

Kosher salt

1 recipe Basic Pizza Dough (page 60)

Cornmeal for dusting

12 oz/280 g Fontina cheese, shredded into 2 cups/230 g

In a large sauté pan over medium-low heat, heat the olive oil. Add the shallots and cook until softened, 5 to 8 minutes.

Meanwhile, remove the Swiss chard stems from the leaves, chop coarsely, and add them to the shallots. Stack the chard leaves, roll them up lengthwise, and slice crosswise into strips about ½ in/12 mm wide. Chop the mixed greens. Add all of the greens with water still clinging to the leaves to the pan. The pan will be very full. Cover it for a few minutes, then remove the lid and toss the greens with tongs to coat with the shallot mixture. When the greens are wilted, sprinkle with the red pepper flakes (if using) and season with salt. Cover and cook, stirring occasionally, until the greens are almost tender, about 8 minutes.

Reduce the heat to low and simmer until all of the moisture is gone, about 3 minutes longer. Remove from the heat and set aside.

*continued*

Preheat the oven to 450°F/230°C/gas 8 and put a pizza stone or heavy-bottomed baking sheet/tray in it to heat.

To assemble the pizzas, flatten the first ball of dough on a surface dusted with cornmeal. Using a rolling pin, roll out the dough into a circle to roughly 12 in/30 cm in diameter and about ¼ in/6 mm thick. Dust a pizza paddle or baking sheet/tray with cornmeal and transfer the pizza dough onto it. Working very quickly, spoon half of the greens mixture over the dough round, spreading it with the back of the spoon to cover and leaving a ½-in/12-mm border. Sprinkle with half of the cheese. Slide the pizza from the paddle directly into the oven onto the pizza stone or baking sheet/tray and bake until the crust is golden brown and the cheese is bubbly and golden, about 15 minutes. Cut the pizza into narrow wedges and serve at once. Repeat to make the second pizza.

**Wine Bite Idea**

There are many variations and combinations of ingredients to use when making your own pizza, depending on your taste and what you have on hand. Experimenting with them is all part of the delicious fun.

Here are a few scrumptious pizza combos to try:
- Caramelized leeks, goat cheese, and sweet Italian sausage
- Sautéed spinach, mozzarella cheese, and prosciutto
- Slow-cooked tomatoes, taleggio cheese, and sautéed wild mushrooms
- Slow-cooked onions and roasted peppers, mozzarella cheese, and pancetta
- Sautéed Swiss chard, Parmesan cheese, and prosciutto

# pizza with zucchini caponata & feta

**makes two 12-in/30.5-cm pizzas**

Caponata is usually made with eggplant/aubergine, but this earthy version made with zucchini/courgettes is quite excellent. In addition to being a delicious pizza topping, caponata makes a wonderful hors d'oeuvre to serve with crispy pita bread or a tangy accompaniment to grilled lamb or steak. This pizza pairs beautifully with a good red Zinfandel or a Rioja.

Zucchini Caponata:

3 medium zucchini/courgettes, trimmed

3 tbsp olive oil

1 red onion, chopped

1 cup/170 g canned plum tomatoes,
    coarsely chopped, with their juices

½ cup/70 g Kalamata olives, pitted and chopped

1 tbsp capers, rinsed and drained

1 tbsp balsamic vinegar

1 tsp sugar

Freshly ground black pepper

1 recipe Basic Pizza Dough (page 60)

Cornmeal for dusting

½ cup/70 g crumbled feta cheese

To make the caponata: Quarter the zucchini/courgettes lengthwise and cut into ½-in/ 12-mm pieces.

In a large skillet, heat 2 tbsp of the olive oil over medium heat. Add the zucchini/courgettes and sauté until golden, about 10 minutes. Using a slotted spoon, transfer to a plate and set aside.

Add the remaining 1 tbsp olive oil to the pan and reduce the heat to medium-low. Add the onion and cook until softened, about 3 minutes. Add the tomatoes and their juices and cook, stirring occasionally, until the juices thicken slightly, about 10 minutes. Return the zucchini/courgettes to the pan and add the olives, capers, vinegar, sugar, and pepper to taste. Reduce the heat to low and simmer, stirring occasionally, until the vegetables are tender and the flavors have blended, about 15 minutes. Taste and adjust the seasoning, if necessary. Set the caponata aside.

Preheat the oven to 450°F/230°C/gas 8 and put a pizza stone or heavy-duty baking sheet/tray in it to heat.

To assemble the pizzas, flatten the first ball of dough on a work surface dusted with cornmeal. Using a rolling pin, roll out the dough into a circle roughly 12 in/30 cm in diameter and about ¼ inch/6 mm thick. Dust a pizza paddle or baking sheet/tray with cornmeal and transfer the pizza dough onto it. Working very quickly, spoon half of the caponata over the dough round, spreading it with the back of the spoon to cover and leaving a ½-in/12-mm border. Sprinkle with half of the cheese. Slide the pizza from the paddle directly into the oven onto the hot pizza stone or baking sheet/tray and bake until the crust is golden brown and the cheese is bubbly and golden, about 15 minutes. Cut the pizza into narrow wedges and serve at once. Repeat to make the second pizza.

**Make-Ahead:** You can make the caponata up to 5 days ahead. Store tightly covered in the refrigerator.

# leek & roquefort cheese tartlets

**makes eight 5-in/12-cm square tartlets; serves 8 to 16**

Roquefort cheese and leeks are a luscious combination, and they mingle tastefully in every sense of the word in these rustic but elegant free-form tartlets made with puff pastry. Both Cabernet Sauvignon and red Zinfandel pair well with the pungent cheese flavor in these tarts.

1 tbsp unsalted butter

3 large leeks, rinsed and finely chopped

Kosher salt and freshly ground black pepper

1¼ cups/170 g Roquefort cheese, crumbled

½ cup/120 ml crème fraîche

One 17.3-oz/495-g package puff pastry
 (2 sheets), thawed if frozen

Fresh thyme sprigs for garnish

Melt the butter in a frying pan over medium-low heat. Add the leeks, season with salt and pepper, and sauté until softened but not browned, about 5 minutes. Remove from the heat and let cool. Transfer the leeks to a large bowl, add the cheese and crème fraîche, and stir gently to mix.

Roll out each pastry sheet on a lightly floured work surface into a 10-in/25-cm square. Cut each sheet into four squares. Using a small knife, score a ½-in/12-mm border around the inside edges of each square, being careful not to cut through the pastry. Arrange the squares on two rimmed baking sheets/trays.

Position one rack in the top third of the oven and another rack in the bottom third of the oven and preheat to 400°F/200°C/gas 6. Spoon the filling over the pastry squares, leaving a ½-in/12-mm border. Bake for 12 minutes. Rotate the baking sheets and continue to bake until the crusts are puffed and golden and the filling is cooked through, about 10 minutes more. Garnish the tarts with the thyme sprigs and serve.

# shiitake mushroom tart

**serves 6 to 8**

A savory mushroom tart is one of my favorite dishes to serve for almost any occasion—meaty, deep-flavored mushrooms in a melting, flaky crust are a knockout combination. Cut wedges from the pan and serve warm or at room temperature. This tart is very nice with Pinot Noir.

Pastry Dough:

1 cup/130 g unbleached all-purpose/plain flour, plus more for dusting

½ tsp salt

5 tbsp/70 g cold unsalted butter, cut into pieces

1½ tsp vegetable shortening/vegetable lard, chilled

¼ cup/60 ml ice water, or as needed

2 tbsp unsalted butter

2 large shallots, finely chopped

12 oz/340 g fresh shiitake mushrooms, stemmed, caps cut into strips about ¼ in/6 mm wide

1 tsp chopped fresh thyme

Kosher salt and freshly ground black pepper

½ cup/60 g freshly shredded Gruyère cheese

3 large eggs

1½ cups/360 ml half-and-half/half cream

To make the pastry dough: In a food processor, combine the 1 cup/130 g flour, salt, butter, and shortening/lard and pulse four or five times until the mixture resembles coarse meal. With the machine running, slowly add about 3 tbsp of the ice water. The dough should begin to mass on the blade. If not, add more water a drop at a time just until the dough holds together. Do not overmix.

Turn the dough out onto a lightly floured work surface. Flatten it with the palm of your hand, dust lightly with flour, and wrap in plastic wrap/cling film. Refrigerate until chilled, 1 or 2 hours.

On a clean work surface lightly dusted with flour, roll the dough out into a 12-in/30-cm circle about ½ in/12 mm thick. Carefully lift the dough and press it into a 9-in/23-cm quiche or tart pan/flan tin with removable bottom. Trim the edges of the dough and crimp with a fork or your fingertips.

Preheat the oven to 400°F/200°C/gas 6. Line the tart shell with aluminum foil and weight with pastry weights or dried beans. Bake for 10 minutes, then remove the foil and weights and bake until golden, about 10 minutes longer. Remove from the oven and reduce the oven temperature to 375°F/190°C/gas 5.

Meanwhile, melt the butter in a skillet over medium heat. Add the shallots and cook until golden, about 5 minutes. Add the mushrooms, thyme, and salt and pepper to taste and cook until the mushrooms are tender and lightly browned, about 8 minutes.

Spread the mushroom mixture in the tart shell and sprinkle the cheese over it. In a bowl, whisk together the eggs and half-and-half/half cream and pour into the tart.

Bake the tart until the filling is fairly firm and is beginning to brown, about 35 to 40 minutes. Serve warm or at room temperature.

# swiss chard, mushroom & chorizo frittata

**serves 6 to 8**

Although frittatas are often thought of as breakfast or brunch dishes, they are quite wonderful to serve with wine, either warm or at room temperature. Chopped chorizo adds a spicy kick to this wine bite. Light, simple whites such as Chardonnay, Muscadet, or Sauvignon Blanc always go well with egg dishes.

Olive oil cooking spray

3 tbsp unsalted butter

2 shallots, finely chopped

1 lb/455 g Swiss chard, stemmed and rinsed

1 cup/85 g finely chopped shiitake mushrooms

7 large eggs

½ cup/60 g freshly shredded Gruyère
  or Comté cheese

½ cup/60 g freshly shredded
  white Cheddar cheese

3 tbsp freshly grated Parmesan cheese

⅓ cup/40 g finely chopped chorizo

Kosher salt and freshly ground black pepper

Preheat the oven to 350°F/180°C/gas 4. Coat a 9-by-12-in/23-by-30-cm baking dish with cooking spray and set aside.

In a large skillet or sauté pan, melt 2 tbsp of the butter over medium heat. Add the shallots and cook until softened, about 5 minutes. Add the chard to the pan, stir well, and reduce the heat to low. Cook, tossing occasionally, until wilted, 7 to 8 minutes. Remove from the heat and let cool. Chop the chard coarsely and set aside.

Wipe out the skillet and melt the remaining 1 tbsp butter over medium heat. Add the mushrooms and cook, stirring occasionally, until golden brown, about 5 minutes.

In a large bowl, beat the eggs with a whisk until frothy. Add the Gruyère and Cheddar cheeses and season with 2 tbsp of the Parmesan cheese and stir to combine. Stir in the chard, mushrooms, and chorizo and season with salt and pepper. Pour the mixture into the prepared pan, sprinkle the top with the remaining 1 tbsp Parmesan cheese, and bake until golden brown, about 20 minutes. Remove from the oven and let the frittata cool for about 10 minutes. Slice into squares and serve warm or at room temperature.

## Chapter 5

# BRUSCHETTA, TOASTS & SANDWICHES

Breads, Toasts & Sandwiches
with Savory Toppings & Tasty Fillings

# basic bruschetta

**makes 12 toasts; serves 4 to 6**

Bruschetta are simply grilled crusty bread slices rubbed with garlic and brushed with olive oil. They can be prepared on a charcoal or gas grill, in a grill pan, or in the oven for the desired crunch and a little pleasant charred flavor. Cook as many slices as will fit in a single layer and turn them only once, until they are nicely grill-marked or golden brown and crispy.

Six ½-in/12-mm slices country
   or sourdough bread
3 large cloves garlic,
   peeled and cut in half lengthwise
About ½ cup/120 ml olive oil

To grill the bruschetta, prepare a medium-hot fire for direct grilling in a charcoal grill/ barbecue, preheat a gas grill to medium-high, or heat a stove-top grill pan over medium heat. Arrange the bread slices in a single layer on the grill rack or in the pan and grill, turning once, until they are golden brown and crispy and slightly charred around the edges, about 3 minutes per side. Transfer to a platter. Rub the garlic halves over one side of the bread and brush lightly with the olive oil.

To make the bruschetta in the oven, preheat to 450°F/230°C/gas 8. Arrange the bread slices in a single layer on a baking sheet/tray and bake, turning once, until golden brown and crispy, about 3 minutes per side. Transfer to a platter. Rub the garlic halves over one side of the bread and brush lightly with the olive oil.

Cut each slice in half and serve.

# bruschetta with figs, prosciutto & arugula

**makes 12 toasts; serves 4 to 6**

What could be better than grilled bruschetta topped with the salty-sweet flavors of prosciutto and figs with a few leaves of fresh arugula/rocket from the garden? Fresh figs have a very short growing season, usually late summer through mid-fall, so take full advantage of them while they are around. Try this bruschetta with a Pinot Noir or chilled rosé.

3 figs, cut into quarters or eighths,
   depending on size

2 tbsp extra-virgin olive oil,
   plus more for drizzling (optional)

1 tbsp balsamic vinegar

12 thin slices prosciutto

12 Basic Bruschetta (facing page)

12 small arugula/rocket leaves, rinsed and dried

In a bowl, toss the figs together with the 2 tbsp olive oil and vinegar.

Lay a slice of prosciutto on each bruschetta. Arrange the figs and arugula/rocket leaves on top. Drizzle with a bit more of the olive oil, if desired, and serve at once.

# bruschetta with sautéed escarole

**makes 12 toasts; serves 4 to 6**

Warm, sautéed greens are terrific over grilled bruschetta. This is a nice light snack that goes beautifully with a glass of wine. Try with a Pinot Noir or chilled rosé.

1 head escarole/Batavian endive
   (about 1 lb/455 g), cored and cut crosswise
   into strips about ½ in/12 mm wide

2 tbsp olive oil

2 cloves garlic, minced

3 anchovy fillets, minced

2 tbsp capers, rinsed, drained, and chopped

12 Kalamata olives, pitted and chopped

Freshly ground black pepper

12 Basic Bruschetta (page 76)

½ cup/60 g freshly grated Parmesan cheese

In a large pot, bring ½ cup/120 ml of lightly salted water to a boil over high heat. Add the escarole/Batavian endive, reduce the heat to medium, cover, and cook until tender, 12 to 15 minutes. Drain the escarole in a colander, reserving ¼ cup/60 ml of the cooking liquid. Press on the greens to remove any excess moisture.

In a large skillet, heat the olive oil over medium heat. Add the garlic and cook, stirring, until fragrant, about 1 minute. Using a wooden spoon, stir in the anchovies, using the back of the spoon to mash them into a paste. Add the capers, olives, greens, and reserved cooking liquid. Reduce the heat to low and cook, stirring occasionally, until the mixture is heated throughout and to allow the flavors to blend, about 10 minutes. Remove from the heat and season with pepper.

Spread the bruschetta with the vegetable mixture, sprinkle a bit of Parmesan cheese over each toast, and serve.

**Make-Ahead:** The vegetable mixture can be made ahead of time. It will keep, tightly covered in the refrigerator, for up to 2 days. Bring to room temperature and reheat gently before assembling the bruschetta.

**Wine Bite Idea:**

There are many delicious combinations of ingredients to use as toppings for bruschetta. Let what looks best at the market be your guide. Here are just a few suggestions:

- Roasted fennel, prosciutto, and freshly grated Parmesan cheese
- Chopped fresh tomatoes, black olives, and ricotta cheese
- Steamed asparagus, mozzarella cheese, and anchovies
- Roasted zucchini/courgettes, toasted pine nuts, and chopped fresh mint
- Grilled eggplant/aubergine, chopped tomatoes, and chopped fresh basil

# parmesan toasts with swiss chard & chickpeas

**makes 16 toasts; serves 6 to 8**

Swiss chard and chickpeas are a winning combination. You can improvise on the beans-and-greens theme to seemingly endless delight for the appetite: try baby spinach and white beans or watercress and black beans. An Italian white, such as Pinot Grigio, or a hearty red Chianti will complement the toasts beautifully.

About ½ baguette, cut into 16 slices
  about ¼ in/6 mm thick
3 large cloves garlic, peeled
  and cut in half lengthwise
About ¼ cup/60 ml olive oil, plus 2 tbsp
¼ cup/30 g freshly grated Parmesan cheese

1 lb/455g Swiss chard
One 15½-oz/445-g can chickpeas,
  rinsed and drained
2 tbsp dry white wine
Pinch of red pepper flakes
Kosher salt and freshly ground black pepper

Preheat the oven to 400°F/200°C/gas 6.

Arrange the bread slices in a single layer on a baking sheet/tray. Rub the garlic halves over one side of the bread and brush lightly with the ¼ cup/60 ml olive oil. Sprinkle the cheese over each slice. Bake until golden brown and crispy, about 5 minutes.

Trim the chard stems and cut crosswise into small pieces. Chop the leaves into ½-in/12-mm strips. Heat 1 tbsp olive oil in a large skillet or sauté pan over medium heat. Sauté the chard stems until soft, about 8 to 10 minutes. Add the chard leaves and sauté until wilted, about 3 minutes. Transfer to a bowl.

In the same pan, heat the remaining 1 tbsp olive oil over medium heat. Add the chickpeas, wine, red pepper flakes, and salt and black pepper to taste and sauté until the wine is reduced and the chickpeas are heated through, about 5 minutes. Return the chard mixture to the pan and toss to mix well.

Spoon the Swiss chard mixture over the toasts and serve at once.

# garlic toasts with cherry tomatoes, basil & goat cheese

**makes 16 toasts; serves 6 to 8**

Although this recipe has been done before in many ways, there is still nothing better to eat than a garlicky toast slathered with goat cheese and topped with garden-fresh cherry tomatoes and basil on a warm summer evening. Serve with a chilled summery white wine, like Sauvignon Blanc or Chardonnay.

2 cups/340 g cherry tomatoes, preferably a mix of red and yellow, stemmed and halved

2 tbsp thinly sliced fresh basil

1 tbsp extra-virgin olive oil

About ½ baguette, cut into 16 slices about ¼ in/6 mm thick

3 large cloves garlic, peeled and cut in half lengthwise

About ¼ cup/60 ml olive oil

3 oz/90 g mild goat cheese, at room temperature

In a bowl, combine the tomatoes, basil, and extra-virgin olive oil and toss to mix well. Let the mixture stand at room temperature for at least 30 minutes and up to 1 hour.

Preheat the oven to 400°F/200°C/gas 6.

Arrange the bread slices in a single layer on a baking sheet/tray. Rub the garlic halves over one side of the bread and brush lightly with the olive oil. Bake until golden brown and crispy, about 5 minutes.

Spread each toast with the goat cheese, top with a spoonful of the tomato mixture, and serve at once.

# polenta crostini with wild mushroom sauté

**makes 2 dozen generous 2-in/5-cm squares or triangles; serves 6 to 8**

Although some may think that preparing polenta is a daunting task, it's actually very simple—mostly a matter of patient stirring—and extra easy to work with if you make it ahead of time and let it chill. Firm polenta cut into two- or three-bite triangles or squares holds together beautifully for sautéing and spreading with any of boundless possibilities for toppings. It's fantastic here with a jumble of sautéed wild mushrooms. These warm chunks of traditional Italian cornmeal crostini are excellent with either a white or red Burgundy wine.

Polenta:

1½ tbsp unsalted butter, plus more for greasing

1 tsp kosher salt

1½ cups/210 g fine yellow cornmeal

4 tbsp/60 ml olive oil, or more as needed

1 lb/455 g assorted wild mushrooms,
   such as cremini/brown mushrooms,
   chanterelles, morels, and shiitake,
   brushed clean, stemmed, and thinly sliced

2 shallots, finely diced

2 tbsp chopped fresh flat-leaf parsley

2 tbsp chopped fresh thyme

To make the polenta: In a large, heavy saucepan, combine 1 qt/960 ml water with the 1½ tbsp butter and salt. Bring to a boil over medium-high heat. Pour in the cornmeal very slowly, stirring constantly with a wooden spoon. When all of the cornmeal has been added, reduce the heat to low. Continue cooking and stirring until the mixture is thick, smooth, and pulls away from the side of the pan, about 15 to 20 minutes.

Spread the polenta evenly in a buttered 9-by-13-in/23-by-33-cm baking pan. Let cool completely, then cover with plastic wrap/cling film and refrigerate until ready to use.

Cut the chilled polenta into 24 squares or triangles. In a large skillet, heat 3 tbsp of the olive oil over medium heat. Working in batches, fry the polenta squares, turning once with a spatula, until lightly browned on both sides, about 2 minutes per side. Add more olive oil to the frying pan as needed. Keep the polenta warm in a low (225°F/110°C/gas ¼) oven until ready to serve.

Heat the remaining 1 tbsp olive oil in a large skillet over medium-high heat. Add the mushrooms and sauté just until softened, about 5 minutes, adding a little more olive oil if needed to prevent sticking. Stir in the shallots, parsley, and thyme and sauté until the mushrooms are tender, about 5 more minutes. Spoon the warm mushroom mixture over the polenta bites and serve at once.

**Make-Ahead:** The polenta will keep, covered in the refrigerator, for up to 3 days. Cut into pieces when you are ready to fry and serve.

**Wine Bite Idea**

Polenta is very good topped with other ingredients. Here are a few others to try.

- Sautéed mixed greens and mascarpone cheese
- Sautéed leeks and Gorgonzola cheese
- Sautéed savoy cabbage with crumbled sweet sausage

# smoked salmon
# & lemon crème fraîche finger sandwiches

**makes 12 or 16 finger sandwiches; serves 6 to 8**

These lovely little sandwiches, made with tangy lemon crème fraîche and thin slices of bread, smoked salmon, and cucumber, may technically be considered tea sandwiches, but I prefer them with wine. Try them with a glass of rosé, white wine, or a Champagne cocktail and I think you will agree.

½ cup/120 ml crème fraîche

1 tbsp fresh lemon juice

1 tbsp capers, rinsed and drained

1 tbsp chopped fresh dill

Freshly ground black pepper

8 thin slices rye, white, or whole-wheat/
   wholemeal bread, crusts trimmed

12 thin slices smoked salmon

12 thin slices cucumber

In a small bowl, stir together the crème fraîche, lemon juice, capers, dill, and pepper to taste. Spread over 4 slices of the bread. Arrange the salmon and cucumber over the spread.

Top with the remaining bread slices. Quarter each sandwich into triangles or squares, or cut lengthwise into three rectangles. Serve at once.

# grilled manchego cheese & serrano ham sandwich bites

**makes 16 squares; serves 6 to 8**

This is about as sophisticated as a grilled cheese sandwich can get. Your guests will love these delicious bites of decadence. These sandwiches, composed of Spanish specialty ham and cheese, call for a glass of Spanish Tempranillo.

2 tbsp unsalted butter, at room temperature

8 slices Italian country-style, sourdough, or olive bread (¼ in/6 mm thick)

8 oz/225 g (2 cups) Manchego cheese (see Note), thinly sliced

8 oz/225 g thinly sliced Serrano ham (*jamón serrano*) (see Note)

Butter one side of each slice of bread. Put 4 slices, buttered-side down, on a work surface. Top the bread slices with half of the sliced cheese. Top the cheese with the sliced ham, dividing it equally. Top with the remaining cheese, then the remaining 4 bread slices, buttered-side up.

Heat a large nonstick skillet over medium heat. Working in batches if necessary to avoid crowding, arrange the sandwiches in the skillet. Cover and cook until golden brown on the first side and the cheese has begun to melt, about 3 minutes. Turn the sandwiches with a spatula, and press to flatten them slightly. Cook until golden brown on the second side and the cheese is soft and creamy. Cut each sandwich into quarters and serve at once.

**Note:** You can find Manchego at almost any good cheese store as well as many supermarkets and specialty-food stores. Serrano ham, one of Spain's several prized types of dry-cured *jamón*, is sold at most of the places you find prosciutto: your local butcher shop or *salumeria*, gourmet food stores, and Spanish and Latin markets.

# buttermilk biscuit bites

**makes 20 small biscuits**

These tasty little biscuits are wonderful filled with almost anything—honey-baked ham and sweet butter, smoked turkey and chutney, or Spicy Chicken Salad (page 129). An elegant French Sancerre or Pinot Blanc is the thing to drink with these.

2 cups/255 g unbleached all-purpose/
    plain flour

1 tbsp baking powder

1 tsp baking soda/bicarbonate of soda

1 tsp kosher salt

5 tbsp/70 g chilled unsalted butter, cut into pieces

¾ cup/180 ml plus 2 tbsp buttermilk

Thinly sliced ham/gammon, smoked turkey,
    or chicken salad for serving

Preheat the oven to 450°F/230°C/gas 8.

In a large bowl, whisk together the flour, baking powder, baking soda/bicarbonate of soda, and salt. Sprinkle the butter pieces over the flour mixture and, using a pastry blender or your fingertips, cut it into the mixture until it resembles coarse meal. (Alternatively, put the dry ingredients in a food processor and process to mix, then add the butter pieces and pulse to mix until the mixture resembles coarse meal. Transfer to a large bowl.)

Add the buttermilk and gently stir until the mixture forms a rough mass. Using your hands, gather the dough into a ball.

Transfer the dough to a lightly floured work surface and knead for about 1 minute. Pat or roll the dough out to form a rectangle about ¾ in/2 cm thick. Using a biscuit cutter dusted with flour, cut the dough into 1-in/2.5-cm rounds. Gather up the dough scraps and repeat to make more biscuits.

Arrange the biscuits about 1 in/2.5 cm apart on an ungreased baking sheet/tray and bake until golden brown, 7 to 9 minutes. Remove from the oven and transfer to a wire rack to cool. Split the biscuits crosswise in half. Add the desired fillings and serve at once.

## Chapter 6

# FRIED BITES

Decadent, Crunchy Bites That are
Finger-Licking Good

# sweet potato fritters

**serves 4 to 6**

These terrific sweet potato fritters are a snap to make and they're fantastic with Ginger-Soy Dipping Sauce (page 123). Italian whites such as Pinot Grigio and Tocai Friulano are good accompaniments to these crunchy fritters as well as the decadent Buttermilk-Fried Vidalia Onion Rings (page 97) and the earthy, savory Eggplant Chips (page 98).

> 4 medium sweet potatoes, scrubbed but unpeeled,
>    ends trimmed
> 1 cup/130 g unbleached all-purpose/plain flour
> Kosher salt and freshly ground black pepper
> 2 large eggs
> Corn or canola oil for frying

Bring a large pot of salted water to a boil. Add the potatoes and simmer until tender, 20 to 25 minutes. Drain and let cool. When cool enough to handle, cut the potatoes into ¼-in/6-mm slices.

Put the flour in a small bowl and season with salt and pepper. Put the eggs in another small bowl and whisk until frothy.

Pour oil to a depth of 1 in/2.5 cm into a heavy-bottomed frying pan and heat until hot but not smoking. Working in batches, dip the potato slices in the egg and then the flour mixture and fry until golden brown, 3 to 4 minutes on each side. Transfer to paper towels/absorbent paper to drain. Keep warm in a low oven while you repeat to fry the remaining fritters. Serve warm.

**Make-Ahead:** The potatoes can be cooked and sliced up to 2 hours ahead of time. Cover and set aside at room temperature.

# fried stuffed zucchini flowers

**makes 12 stuffed blossoms; serves 4 to 6**

Zucchini flowers are the vivid golden yellow blossoms that grow on the ends of zucchini/courgette plants, both right out of the baby fruits (these are the female blossoms) and the stems (male). When stuffed with cheese, dipped in batter, and lightly fried, the tender flowers are downright addictive. Celebrate spring with a platter of these slightly floral-tasting fried delicacies and glasses of chilled Champagne or sparkling wine.

12 large zucchini/courgette flowers

3 ¼ oz/90 g fontina
  or mozzarella cheese

2 large egg yolks

1 cup/240 ml ice water

1 cup/130 g unbleached all-purpose/plain flour

Corn or canola oil for frying

Kosher salt and freshly ground black pepper

Open the top of each blossom and carefully remove the stamen inside the flower. Rinse under cold water and lay out on a clean kitchen towel to dry for at least 1 hour.

Slice the cheese into pieces about 1 in/2.5 cm long. Open the ends of the flowers again and put a piece of cheese inside each. Twist the ends to keep the cheese enclosed. In a bowl, lightly beat the egg yolks, then add the ice water and flour and stir until smooth.

Place a wire rack on a baking sheet/tray and set aside. Pour oil into a deep sauté pan to a depth of 1 in/2.5 cm and heat over medium-high heat until hot but not smoking. Dip each blossom into the batter, holding onto the twisted end with tongs. Carefully lay the blossoms on their sides in the hot oil. Fry on the first side for 30 seconds, then turn and fry until golden brown all over and the cheese is melted, about 30 seconds longer. Transfer to the wire rack to drain.

Sprinkle with salt and pepper and serve warm.

# fried watercress sprigs

**makes 2 dozen bites; serves 6 to 8**

Fried vegetables such as broccoli, broccoli rabe, and green beans have become very popular treats frequently served in wine bars. Watercress leaves are another delectable bite to savor with a glass of wine. Look for sprigs with sturdy stems that can be used as a handle to pick up the watercress after it's fried. Tangy-flavored Albariño is very good with these crisp-tender bites.

1 large bunch of watercress (for 24 sturdy sprigs)
½ cup/60 g prepared tempura mix (see Note)
Kosher salt
Canola oil for frying
Remoulade Sauce (page 119),
   Anchovy-Tarragon Mayonnaise (page 118),
   or your favorite sauce for serving

Choose the best pieces of watercress—ones that have a good amount of leaves and a sturdy long stem. Rinse them and lay them out to dry between paper towels/absorbent paper.

In a bowl, combine the tempura mix and ⅔ cup/165 ml water and season with salt. The batter should be thin (so the leaves will be well coated) but not watery.

Pour oil into a heavy-bottomed saucepan to a depth of 1 in/2.5 cm and heat over medium-high heat until hot but not smoking. Fry in batches of 2 or 3 sprigs as you go, and do not overcrowd the pan. Using tongs, pick up a watercress stem and dip the leaf end into the batter, sweeping it to coat. Let the excess batter fall back into the bowl and then lower the coated stem into the hot oil. Fry until lightly browned, about 15 seconds. Transfer to a wire rack to drain for a few minutes, then transfer to a serving plate. Repeat to fry all of the watercress, piling the sprigs attractively on the plate. Serve at once with the sauce of your choice.

**Note:** Packaged tempura mix is available in Asian markets and in the international foods section of supermarkets.

# buttermilk-fried vidalia onion rings

**makes 2 dozen bites; serves 6 to 8**

Sweet Vidalia onions used to have a very short growing season—late April through the end of May—but recently, by virtue of advanced farming technology, their availability has been extended through the summer months. Take full advantage of special extra-sweet onions and make some scrumptious onion rings for your next party. A light, citrusy California Chardonnay or a dry Pinot Grigio would pair well with these.

2 large Vidalia onions

1 cup/130 g unbleached all-purpose/plain flour

1 tsp baking powder

1 tbsp sugar

Pinch of cayenne pepper

Kosher salt

2 cups/480 ml buttermilk

Corn or canola oil for frying

Cut the onions into ½-in/12-mm slices and separate into rings.

In a large bowl, whisk together the flour, baking powder, sugar, and cayenne pepper. Season with salt. Add the buttermilk and whisk until smooth.

Pour oil into a deep, heavy-bottomed saucepan or Dutch oven to a depth of 2 in/5 cm and heat over high heat until hot but not smoking.

Working in batches, dip the onion rings in the batter, letting the excess drip back into the bowl, and fry until golden brown, 2 to 3 minutes. Transfer to paper towels/absorbent paper to drain and keep warm in a low oven while frying the rest. Sprinkle with additional salt and serve at once.

# eggplant chips

These crunchy chips are a big crowd pleaser. The key to making them is to replenish the bread crumbs while you're prepping the eggplant for frying, so they don't get soggy. Try a crisp Muscadet or an Italian white wine such as Pinot Grigio or Orvieto with these.

1 large eggplant/aubergine
   (about 1½ lb/680 g), trimmed
1 large egg
1 cup/240 ml whole milk
1½ cups/190 g unbleached
   all-purpose/plain flour

3 cups/170 g fine fresh bread crumbs
Corn or canola oil for frying
Kosher salt and freshly ground black pepper

Peel the eggplant/aubergine, slice it very thinly, lengthwise, and then cut into 2-in-/5-cm-wide strips.

In a large bowl, whisk together the egg and milk and set aside.

Put the flour in a large plastic bag. Working in batches, add the vegetable pieces and shake until they are well coated. Put them in the bowl with the egg mixture and stir gently until they are completely coated.

Put about one-third of the bread crumbs on a plate. Dip the vegetable pieces into the crumbs, pressing hard so the crumbs stick. Shake gently to remove any excess. Discard the bread crumbs as they become wet and replace with dry crumbs until all of the eggplant/aubergine is coated.

Pour oil into a heavy-bottomed frying pan to a depth of 2 in/5 cm and heat until hot but not smoking. Add the vegetable pieces a handful at a time and fry until golden brown, about 1 minute. Transfer to paper towels/absorbent paper to drain. Sprinkle with salt and pepper and serve at once.

# fried mozzarella bites

**serves 6 to 8**

The secret for achieving just the right coating on these fantastic fried mozzarella balls that are golden on the outside and meltingly gorgeous on the inside is to roll them in a bit of flour before dipping them in egg and bread crumbs, and chilling them a bit before frying so they don't cook too fast.

12 mozzarella balls *(bocconcini)*, about 1½ in/4 cm in diameter

2 cups/230 g unbleached all-purpose/plain flour

Kosher salt and freshly ground black pepper

3 large eggs, lightly beaten

2 cups/110 g fresh bread crumbs

Canola oil for frying

Slice the mozzarella balls in half, place in a colander in the sink, and let drain for 2 hours. Line a baking sheet/tray with wax/greaseproof paper and set aside.

Whisk together the flour and salt and pepper to taste in a shallow bowl. Put the eggs and bread crumbs in separate shallow bowls. Dip each piece of cheese in the flour, then in the egg, then in the bread crumbs, shaking off any excess after each step. Put the cheese balls on the prepared baking sheet/tray and refrigerate until chilled, about 30 minutes.

Pour oil into a heavy-bottomed skillet or frying pan to a depth of 2 in/5 cm and heat until hot but not smoking. Working in batches, fry the cheese balls until golden, 1 to 2 minutes. Using a slotted spoon, transfer to paper towels/absorbent paper to drain. Repeat to fry the remaining cheese. Serve at once.

**Wine Bite Idea**

The fried mozza' balls are quite delicious eaten on their own, but you will also receive raves if you serve them with warm tomato sauce or pesto sauce for dipping.

## Chapter 7

# SEABOARD

## SEAFOOD

Savory & Scrumptious Fish
& Shellfish Bites

# ginger shrimp cocktail with spicy dipping sauce

**serves 6 to 8**

Shrimp cocktail has been a beloved American party dish for decades. I created this new twist on the popular classic in which the shrimp/prawns are infused with fresh ginger and red pepper flakes, and the dipping sauce is made with sweet (often labeled "Thai style") Asian chili sauce and fresh lime juice. I guarantee you'll agree: it's fantastic. In addition to the usual dry whites that pair well with seafood, Riesling is an interesting choice to try with this dish.

¼ cup/30 g peeled and thinly sliced
   fresh ginger
½ cup/120 ml rice vinegar
2 tbsp sugar
1 tsp red pepper flakes
2 lb/910 g large (16 to 20 count)
   shrimp/prawns

Spicy Dipping Sauce:
¼ cup/60 ml sweet Asian chili sauce
2 tbsp ketchup/tomato sauce
1 tbsp Dijon mustard
2 tbsp fresh lime juice
1 tsp Asian fish sauce (*nam pla*)

In a small saucepan, combine the ginger, vinegar, sugar, and red pepper flakes. Bring to a boil, stirring to dissolve. Transfer to a large bowl and let cool.

Bring a large pot of salted water to a boil. Add the shrimp/prawns and cook until just opaque throughout, about 3 minutes. Drain the shellfish, run under cool water, and peel and devein, leaving the tails on.

Add the shrimp/prawns to the ginger mixture and refrigerate for at least 1 hour and up to 4 hours, stirring occasionally. Drain the shellfish and pat dry. Discard the ginger mixture.

To make the sauce: In a small bowl, stir together the chili sauce, ketchup/tomato sauce, mustard, lime juice, and fish sauce. Taste and adjust the seasoning, if necessary, and refrigerate until ready to serve.

Arrange the shellfish on a large platter or in a bowl and serve with the dipping sauce.

# baked clams with walnuts & herbs

**makes 2 dozen clams on the half shell; serves 6 to 8**

Like oysters, clams on the half shell are wonderful briny treats, but opening them can be very labor intensive, especially when you're hosting. I like to bake whole clams in the oven for a few minutes until they open, and then spoon fresh herbs, nuts, and bacon onto them. After a few more minutes in the oven, these sizzling treats are ready to serve. These rich bites with nuttiness, the fresh taste of the sea, and herbal notes are terrific with a glass of chilled Manzanilla sherry.

24 littleneck clams, scrubbed and rinsed

1 large clove garlic, peeled

¼ cup/30 g chopped walnuts or pecans

1 tbsp capers, rinsed and drained

2 tbsp chopped fresh flat-leaf parsley,
   plus sprigs for garnish

1 tbsp chopped fresh tarragon

2 tbsp olive oil

2 tbsp dried bread crumbs

2 strips bacon/streaky bacon,
   cut into ¼-in/6-mm pieces

Lemon wedges for garnish

Preheat the oven to 500°F/260°C/gas 10.

Put the clams on a baking sheet/tray and bake until they open, 10 to 15 minutes. When cool enough to handle, remove the upper shells and return them to the tray.

Meanwhile, combine the garlic, nuts, capers, 2 tbsp parsley, and tarragon in a food processor and process until minced.

In a skillet, heat the olive oil over medium heat. Add the nut mixture and sauté briefly. Stir in the bread crumbs and cook, stirring, until well blended and toasty, about 5 minutes.

Spoon the topping onto the clams and top with the bacon pieces. Bake until the topping is lightly browned and the bacon is sizzling, about 5 minutes. Arrange on a platter, garnish with lemon wedges and parsley sprigs, and serve at once.

# roasted oysters with shallots, bacon & chives

**makes 2 dozen oysters on the half shell; serves 6 to 8**

There is nothing more festive than serving oysters on the half shell for a party, but shucking them can be difficult. When they're roasted in the oven on a bed of rock salt, their shells open on their own and you can then add an herbed cream sauce and finish baking them. This is a very elegant dish to serve for a special occasion—and special occasions always call for Champagne.

1 tbsp unsalted butter

3 shallots, finely chopped

2 cloves garlic, minced

¾ cup/180 ml dry white wine

¾ cup/180 ml fish stock or clam juice

½ cup/120 ml heavy (whipping)/double cream

3 tbsp chopped fresh chives,
   plus minced chives for garnish

Pinch of freshly grated nutmeg

Kosher salt and freshly ground black pepper

Rock salt

24 medium oysters, scrubbed and chilled

4 strips bacon/streaky bacon,
   each cut into 6 pieces about 1 in/2.5 cm long

Preheat the oven to 400°F/200°C/gas 6.

In a large saucepan, melt the butter over medium heat. Add the shallots and garlic and sauté until softened, about 5 minutes. Add the wine and stock; simmer until reduced by half. Add the cream and simmer, stirring occasionally, until slightly thickened, about 5 minutes. Add the chopped chives and nutmeg. Season with salt and pepper, and simmer for 2 minutes. Keep the mixture warm.

Spread a layer of rock salt over a baking sheet/tray. Set the oysters into the salt, rounded-side down. Roast until the top shells start to loosen and the oysters start to open, about 15 minutes. Remove them from the oven and with a small sharp knife, carefully remove the top shells and detach the oysters, keeping the liquid in the shell. Spoon 1 tbsp of the cream sauce over each oyster and return to the oven for 5 to 7 minutes.

Meanwhile, in a frying pan over medium heat, cook the bacon pieces until just crisp. Using a slotted spoon, transfer to paper towels/absorbent paper to drain.

Garnish each oyster with a piece of bacon and sprinkle with the minced chives. Serve at once.

# chilled mussels vinaigrette

**makes about 32 mussels on the half shell; serves 6 to 8**

The marinated mussels should be chilled for at least 2 hours before spooning them back in their shiny black shells, so plan accordingly. Small mussels from Prince Edward Island are excellent for this dish. These are lovely with chilled Pinot Grigio or Pinot Blanc.

2 tbsp olive oil

3 cloves garlic, thinly sliced

1½ cups/360 ml dry white wine

1½ lb/680 g mussels (about 32), scrubbed, debearded, and rinsed

Mustard Vinaigrette:

½ small yellow onion, coarsely chopped

2 cloves garlic, finely chopped

¼ cup/60 ml dry white wine

1½ tbsp white vinegar

2 tsp Dijon mustard

1 tsp Worcestershire sauce

Dash of hot-pepper sauce

2 tbsp chopped fresh flat-leaf parsley

Kosher salt and freshly ground black pepper

¼ cup/60 ml olive oil

¼ cup/60 ml corn oil

Lemon wedges for garnish

Parsley sprigs for garnish

Heat the olive oil in a large soup pot over medium heat. Add the garlic and sauté for 2 minutes. Add the wine and bring to a boil. Add the mussels, reduce the heat to medium-low, cover, and cook until the mussels open, 6 to 8 minutes. Using a slotted spoon, transfer the mussels to a bowl. Discard any unopened or broken mussels. When cool enough to handle, remove the mussels from their shells and transfer to a bowl. Reserve half of the mussel shells.

To make the vinaigrette: In a food processor, combine the onion, garlic, wine, vinegar, mustard, Worcestershire sauce, hot-pepper sauce, chopped parsley, and salt and black pepper to taste. Process until smooth. With the machine running, pour in the oils very slowly in thin, steady streams. Continue processing until the oils are incorporated and the mixture is emulsified into a smooth vinaigrette. Taste and adjust the seasoning.

Pour about ½ cup/120 ml of the vinaigrette over the mussels and toss gently. Add more vinaigrette as needed. Refrigerate until well chilled, 2 to 3 hours.

Spoon one or two mussels into a mussel shell and transfer to a serving platter garnished with lemon wedges and fresh parsley sprigs.

# mini crab cakes

**serves 6 to 8**

Crab cakes are a delicate business, but the key to making these scrumptious morsels is to chill them for an hour or two before frying them so they don't fall apart. They're terrific with all kinds of accompaniments—Anchovy-Tarragon Mayonnaise (page 118), Remoulade Sauce (page 119), or Dill Sauce (page 120). Try these with a flinty Chablis or a Sancerre.

1 lb/455 g fresh lump crabmeat,
   picked over for cartilage and shell fragments

1 tbsp fresh lemon juice

½ cup/55 g plain dried bread crumbs

1 large egg

5 tbsp/75 g mayonnaise, homemade
   (see page 116) or good-quality commercial

2 green/spring onions,
   white and tender green parts, finely minced

1 tbsp chopped fresh flat-leaf parsley

1 tbsp dry mustard

Salt and freshly ground black pepper

2 tbsp unsalted butter

2 tbsp canola or safflower oil

Place the crabmeat in a bowl, sprinkle with the lemon juice, and toss gently to coat.

In a large bowl, stir together the bread crumbs, egg, mayonnaise, green/spring onions, parsley, and mustard. Season with salt and pepper. Add the crabmeat and stir gently until mixed.

Shape the crab mixture into small patties about 1 in/2.5 cm thick and 2 in/5 cm wide and place on a baking sheet/tray. Cover with plastic wrap/cling film and refrigerate for at least 1 hour and up to 2 hours.

In a large frying pan, melt 1 tbsp of the butter with 1 tbsp of the oil over medium heat. Add half of the crab cakes to the pan and cook, turning once, until golden, 3 to 5 minutes per side. Drain on paper towels/absorbent paper. Heat the remaining butter and oil and repeat to cook the rest of the crab cakes. Serve at once.

# tuna, cucumber & red pepper tartare

**serves 6**

"Sushi-quality" or "sushi-grade" tuna is the key ingredient in this refreshing and elegant dish, which means buy the best and freshest you can find. It may cost more than regular tuna, but the results are well worth it. Chop the tuna on a pristine work surface with a clean knife, toss it with the other ingredients, and let it mellow in the refrigerator for no more than 2 hours. (The tuna's texture will soften if you let it sit any longer.) The tartare is lovely served over a round of fresh cucumber and a crunchy rice or sesame cracker. Choosing a wine to drink with sushi-style dishes can be tricky, but in addition to sake, this is wonderful with Champagne or Prosecco.

1½ lb/680 g sushi-quality tuna

3 tbsp chopped cilantro/fresh coriander

2 tbsp minced shallot

1 tsp peeled and minced fresh ginger

3 tbsp capers, rinsed and drained

1 cucumber, peeled, seeded, and finely diced

½ cup/70 g seeded and diced red bell pepper/capsicum

½ cup/70 g diced red onion

2 tsp extra-virgin olive oil

Kosher salt and freshly ground black pepper

2 tbsp fresh lime juice

Sesame and/or rice crackers and thin rounds of cucumber for serving

Using a very sharp knife, dice the tuna as finely as possible. Transfer to a bowl and add the cilantro/fresh coriander, shallot, ginger, capers, cucumber, bell pepper/capsicum, onion, and olive oil. Mix gently until well combined and season with salt and pepper. Cover and refrigerate until chilled, 1½ to 2 hours, but no longer.

Gently toss the lime juice with the tuna. Serve at once with the cucumber rounds and crackers.

# fish & avocado ceviche

**Serves 6 to 8**

Ceviche is a cold preparation of fish or shellfish that "cooks" the raw seafood with an acidic marinade of citrus juice. Prepare this with the freshest fish you can find and have your fishmonger fillet and skin the fish for you. The ceviche is fabulous with a crisp Muscadet or Sauvignon Blanc.

1½ lb/680 g skinless fish fillets
such as red snapper, sea bass, or flounder,
cut into ¼-in/6-mm cubes

¾ cup/180 ml fresh lemon juice

¾ cup/180 ml fresh lime juice

½ red onion, finely diced

2 green/spring onions, white and tender
green parts, trimmed and finely minced

½ cup/70 g seeded and diced red
bell pepper/capsicum

½ cup/70 g seeded and diced yellow
bell pepper/capsicum

1 jalapeño chile, seeded, deveined, and minced

½ cup/85 g diced plum tomato

1 tbsp capers, rinsed and drained

¼ cup/40 g finely chopped green olives

2 tbsp chopped fresh flat-leaf parsley

Dash of hot-pepper sauce

2 tsp extra-virgin olive oil

Kosher salt and freshly ground black pepper

2 ripe Hass avocados, pitted, peeled,
and cut into ¼-in/6-mm cubes

Put the cubed fish in a nonreactive bowl and pour the lemon and lime juices over it. Mix well, cover, and let marinate in the refrigerator for about 6 hours. Stir occasionally.

In a bowl, combine the red onion, green/spring onions, bell peppers/capsicums, jalapeño, tomato, capers, olives, parsley, hot-pepper sauce, and olive oil. Season with salt and pepper and stir to mix well. Cover and refrigerate for about 6 hours.

Just before serving, drain the fish, discarding the liquid, and transfer to a large bowl. Add the vegetable mixture and the avocados to the fish and mix well. Taste and adjust the seasoning, if necessary. Serve at once.

# chopped egg salad & salmon caviar toasts

**serves 8 to 10**

Simple chopped egg salad becomes something very special when it's topped with red salmon caviar.
A platter of these beautiful, tasty toasts served with flutes of Champagne or sparkling wine hits just
the right festive note.

½ lb/225 g watercress, plus sprigs for garnish

6 large eggs

2 green/spring onions, white and
   tender green parts, minced

2 tbsp mayonnaise, homemade (see page 116)
   or good-quality commercial

1 tsp fresh lemon juice

Kosher salt

Buttered toasts for serving

3 oz/90 g salmon caviar

Remove the large stems from the watercress and rinse well in several changes of cold water.
Spin dry in a salad spinner or pat with a clean towel. Chop the watercress and transfer to a
large bowl.

Put the eggs in a large pot with cold water to cover by about 1 in/2.5 cm. Bring to a boil over
high heat. Remove from the heat, cover, and let stand for 25 minutes. Drain the pot and fill it
again with cold water. Let the eggs stand in the water until they are completely cooled.

Peel the eggs, chop, and add to the bowl with the watercress. Add the green/spring onions,
mayonnaise, and lemon juice. Season with salt and mix well. Taste and adjust the seasoning,
adding a bit more mayonnaise, if necessary. Serve on the buttered toasts topped with a small
spoonful of caviar and a small sprig of watercress for garnish.

# salsa, spreads & sauces for seafood

It's amazing how a delicious, well-made salsa, spread, or sauce can transform ordinary seafood into something very special.

Salsa is usually considered a dip for nachos and tortilla chips, but a homemade salsa made with fresh seasonal ingredients is a knockout accompaniment to shrimp/prawns, crabcakes, chilled mussels, and grilled fish.

Spreads and sauces made with homemade mayonnaise taste fantastic with shrimp/prawns, mussels, crabcakes, and fried, grilled, or poached fish. Homemade mayonnaise is far superior to any commercial brands—it's truly worth the time and effort to make it. All you need is an egg, Dijon mustard, fresh lemon juice, and vegetable oil. Whether you whip up a small batch by hand or a larger amount using a food processor, it is a wonderful base for an anchovy-tarragon mayonnaise, a spicy remoulade sauce, or any number of sauces made with fresh, aromatic herbs.

Easy-to-make sauces made with ingredients like soy sauce, fresh ginger, and lemon or lime juices are good things to make ahead of time and serve with all types of seafood. Shrimp/prawns, grilled scallops, and fish fritters all taste terrific with dipping sauces.

Here are few simple recipes that will enhance every seafood dish that you serve.

# cherry tomato, corn & caper salsa

**makes about 3 cups**

2 ears corn, husked

2 cups/340 g cherry tomatoes,
coarsely chopped

½ red onion, finely diced

2 scallions, trimmed and minced

1½ tbsp capers, drained

1 tbsp balsamic vinegar

1 tsp ground cumin

1 tsp hot-pepper sauce

Kosher salt and freshly ground black pepper

Bring a large pot of water to a boil. Add the corn, return to the boil, and cook for 5 minutes. Lift the corn from the water and set aside to cool. When cool enough to handle, scrape the kernels off the cobs with a small, sharp knife, and transfer to a large bowl.

Add the tomatoes, onion, scallions, capers, vinegar, cumin, and hot-pepper sauce to the corn and toss gently. Season with salt and pepper.

Cover and refrigerate for at least 2 hours before serving. The salsa will keep in the refrigerator, covered, for up to 3 days.

# homemade mayonnaise by hand

**makes 1 cup/240 ml**

1 large egg yolk, at room temperature
Kosher salt and freshly ground black pepper
1 tsp Dijon mustard
1 tsp fresh lemon juice
1 cup/240 ml vegetable or corn oil

In a bowl, whisk together the egg yolk and salt and pepper to taste. Add the mustard and lemon juice and whisk until well combined.

Add the oil very gradually, whisking constantly until all of the oil is incorporated and the sauce is thick and emulsified; this can take up to 5 minutes. If not using the mayonnaise immediately, whisk in 1 tbsp water to stabilize it. The mayonnaise will keep, tightly covered in the refrigerator, for up to 5 days. Bring to room temperature before using.

# homemade mayonnaise by food processor

**makes about 1½ cups/360 ml**

2 large egg yolks, at room temperature

2 tsp Dijon mustard

½ cup/120 ml olive oil

¾ cup/180 ml vegetable or corn oil

2 tsp fresh lemon juice

Kosher salt and freshly ground black pepper

Combine the egg yolks and mustard in the bowl of a food processor. Pulse for 1 or 2 seconds to blend.

With the motor running, gradually add both oils through the feed tube of the food processor in slow, steady streams and process until the sauce is thick and emulsified, about 2 minutes. Add the lemon juice. Season with salt and pepper and pulse just to blend. Taste and adjust the seasoning, if necessary. Spoon the mayonnaise into a serving bowl or airtight container. It will keep, tightly covered in the refrigerator, for up to 5 days. Bring to room temperature before using.

# anchovy-tarragon mayonnaise

**makes about 1 cup/240 ml**

1 cup/240 ml mayonnaise, homemade (see page 116)
or good-quality commercial

2 tsp fresh lemon juice

6 anchovy fillets, finely chopped

1 tbsp chopped fresh tarragon

In a small bowl, stir together the mayonnaise, lemon juice, anchovies, and tarragon. The sauce will keep, covered in the refrigerator, for up to 1 day. Bring to room temperature before using.

# remoulade sauce

**makes about 1 cup/240 ml**

⅔ cup/165 ml mayonnaise, homemade
(see page 116) or good-quality commercial

¼ cup/60 ml Dijon mustard

2 green/spring onions, white and
tender green parts, chopped

2 tbsp finely minced fresh flat-leaf parsley

1 tsp fresh lemon juice

1 tsp Worcestershire sauce

1 tbsp sweet paprika

Dash of hot-pepper sauce

Kosher salt and freshly ground black pepper

In a bowl, whisk together the mayonnaise, mustard, green/spring onions, parsley, lemon juice, Worcestershire sauce, paprika, hot-pepper sauce, and salt and pepper to taste until well blended. Taste and adjust the seasoning, if necessary. The sauce will keep, covered in the refrigerator, for up to 1 day. Bring to room temperature before using.

# dill sauce

........................

**makes about ¾ cup/180 ml**

½ cup/120 ml mayonnaise, homemade (see page 116)
  or good-quality commercial

2 tsp Dijon mustard

2 tbsp chopped fresh dill

2 tsp milk

Pinch of sugar

Combine the mayonnaise, mustard, and dill in a bowl and stir to mix well. Add the milk and sugar and mix again. Taste and adjust the seasoning. The sauce will keep, covered in the refrigerator, for up to 1 day. Bring to room temperature before using.

# watercress sauce

**makes about 1 cup/240 ml**

1 tbsp unsalted butter

1 tbsp chopped shallots

2 tbsp dry white wine

2 tbsp chicken stock

¾ cup/180 ml heavy (whipping)/double cream

1 bunch watercress, stemmed

1 tsp fresh lemon juice

Kosher salt and freshly ground black pepper

In a small saucepan, heat the butter over medium heat. Add the shallots and sauté until golden. Add the wine and cook until almost completely evaporated. Add the chicken stock and cream. Bring to a boil, reduce the heat to medium-low, and simmer until slightly thickened, about 5 minutes. Stir in the watercress. Transfer to a blender and blend until smooth, about 1 minute. Add lemon juice and season with salt and pepper. Taste and adjust the seasonings, if necessary, and pulse just to blend. The sauce should be very light and creamy. Store, covered in the refrigerator, for up to 1 day. Bring to room temperature before using.

# peanut, soy & ginger dipping sauce

**makes about ½ cup/120 ml**

2 tbsp smooth peanut butter

2 tbsp plain low-fat yogurt

2 tbsp soy sauce

1 tbsp fresh lime juice

1 tbsp peeled and finely chopped fresh ginger

½ tsp toasted sesame oil

Dash of hot-pepper sauce

Combine the peanut butter, yogurt, soy sauce, lime juice, ginger, sesame oil, and hot-pepper sauce in a blender and blend until very smooth. Taste and adjust the seasoning, if necessary. The sauce will keep, covered in the refrigerator, for up to 2 days. Bring to room temperature before serving.

# ginger-soy dipping sauce

**makes about ¾ cup/180 ml**

½ cup/120 ml low-sodium soy sauce

2 tbsp rice vinegar

2 tbsp sugar

1 tbsp peeled and minced fresh ginger

2 tbsp minced green/spring onion

Dash of hot-pepper sauce

In a bowl, whisk together the soy sauce, vinegar, sugar, ginger, green/spring onion, and hot-pepper sauce. The sauce will keep, covered in the refrigerator, for up to 2 days. Bring to room temperature before serving.

*Chapter 8*

# MEATS

❖

## HEARTY BITES & MORE TO SERVE WITH GOOD WINE

# chicken satay with peanut dipping sauce

**makes 20 skewers; serves 6 to 8**

Skewers straight from the fire make wonderful appetizers. These bites of barbecued Thai-spiced chicken on a stick are always welcome. *Nam pla*, *sambal oelek*, and lemongrass are available in Asian markets, where you will also find inexpensive bags of bamboo skewers. Wooden skewers for cooking are also available in most well-stocked supermarkets. Grilled dishes always go well with both red and white wines. Either Pinot Noir or Chardonnay would be a good choice.

Marinade:
1 small yellow onion, peeled and quartered
¼ cup/35 g minced lemongrass (see Note)
2 cloves garlic, coarsely chopped
½-in/12-mm piece fresh ginger, peeled and coarsely chopped
¼ cup/50 g firmly packed brown/demerara sugar
3 tbsp soy sauce
3 tbsp fish sauce *(nam pla)*
2 tbsp fresh lime juice
1 tbsp ground coriander
2 tsp ground cumin
½ tsp ground turmeric

1½ lb/680 g skinless, boneless chicken breasts, cut into 20 strips
Vegetable oil cooking spray for grilling

Dipping Sauce:
1 tbsp vegetable oil
1 cup/240 ml unsweetened coconut milk
½ cup/140 g smooth peanut butter
1 tbsp brown/demerara sugar
1 tsp chile paste such as *sambal oelek*
2 tbsp fresh lime juice
2 tbsp chopped peanuts

¼ cup/10 g chopped cilantro/fresh coriander

To make the marinade: In a food processor, combine the onion, lemongrass, garlic, ginger, brown/demerara sugar, soy sauce, fish sauce, lime juice, ground coriander, cumin, and turmeric and process until smooth.

Put the chicken strips in a large zippered plastic bag and pour in the marinade. Seal the bag and massage gently to coat the chicken with the marinade. Let marinate in the refrigerator, turning the bag once or twice, for at least 4 hours or up to overnight.

*continued*

If using wooden skewers, soak twenty of them in cold water for at least 30 minutes. Meanwhile, prepare a medium-hot fire for direct grilling in a charcoal grill/barbecue, or preheat a gas grill to medium-high. Coat the grill rack with cooking oil spray to prevent sticking. Alternatively, preheat the broiler/grill.

To make the dipping sauce: Heat the oil in a saucepan over medium-high heat. Add the coconut milk and bring to a boil, stirring. Whisk in the peanut butter, brown/demerara sugar, and chile paste and return just to a simmer. Remove from the heat and let cool a bit. Transfer the sauce to a blender, add the lime juice, and blend until smooth. Transfer to a small serving bowl and garnish with the peanuts. Set aside.

Drain the skewers. Remove the chicken strips from the marinade and discard the marinade. Thread one chicken strip on each skewer, working the skewer in and out of the middle of the strip vertically so it stays in place during grilling. Nudge the threaded chicken strip gently along the skewer so it fills only half of the skewer, leaving the other half empty so you have a handle to work with.

Wearing an oven mitt or grill glove or using tongs, arrange the skewers directly over the fire. Grill/barbecue, turning once, until the chicken is opaque throughout and nicely grill-marked, about 5 minutes per side. Or slip under the broiler/grill and broil/grill, turning once, until opaque throughout, 5 to 7 minutes per side.

Arrange the satay on a platter, garnish with the cilantro/fresh coriander, and serve at once with the dipping sauce.

**Note:** When purchasing stalks of fresh lemongrass, look for firm stalks. To use, cut off the lower bulb and remove any tough outer leaves. Mince the yellow part of the stalks.

# spicy chicken salad with endive leaves

**makes about 3 dozen hors d'oeuvres**

Crispy leaves of endive/chicory filled with spicy chicken salad make great hors d'oeuvres. The succulent spears are perfect finger food. It's best to make the chicken salad a day ahead of time to give the flavors time to meld and intensify. This is a nice dish to serve for a summer party or picnic with chilled rosé.

1 yellow onion

2 carrots, peeled

2 stalks celery, trimmed

6 fresh flat-leaf parsley sprigs,
  plus ½ cup/15 g chopped parsley

Kosher salt

1½ lb/680 g skinless, boneless
  chicken breasts

½ cup/85 g seeded and finely chopped
  red bell pepper/capsicum

½ cup/120 ml mayonnaise, homemade
  (see page 116) or good-quality commercial

¼ cup/60 ml plain yogurt

1 tbsp chili powder

1 tbsp ground cumin

1 tbsp fresh lime juice

Freshly ground black pepper

½ cup/55 g finely chopped walnuts

3 heads Belgian endive/chicory, separated into leaves
  and leaves cut into 2½- to 3-in/6- to 7.5-cm pieces

Chopped pickled jalapeños for garnish (optional)

Fill a large saucepan with water. Add the onion, carrots, celery, parsley sprigs, and salt to taste and bring to a boil over high heat. Reduce the heat to medium-low, add the chicken, and simmer, partially covered, for 20 minutes. Remove from the heat and let the chicken cool in the cooking liquid.

Using tongs, transfer the chicken to a cutting board and pat dry with paper towels/absorbent paper. Discard the cooking liquid and vegetables. Chop the chicken into small pieces and place in a large bowl. Add the bell pepper/capsicum and toss.

In a medium bowl, combine the mayonnaise, yogurt, chili powder, cumin, and lime juice. Season with salt and pepper and mix well. Fold into the chicken mixture and stir well to combine. Add the walnuts and chopped parsley and toss again. Taste and adjust the seasoning, if necessary. Cover and refrigerate until well chilled, at least 4 hours or up to overnight.

Spoon the chicken salad into the endive/chicory pieces and arrange on a platter. Top each with chopped jalapeños, if desired, and serve at once.

# serving antipasto

Antipasto *literally means "before the meal" in Italian. A traditional antipasto platter is made up of a variety of cured meats, cheeses, olives, and raw fresh vegetables and cooked and marinated vegetables. It is served with bread and bread sticks.*

*For busy hosts who don't have the time to cook or who prefer not to, it is the perfect appetizer or wine bite platter to serve. All it takes is a bit of planning and some smart shopping. Look for the ingredients to create an antipasto platter at gourmet shops, delicatessens, and local Italian and other ethnic specialty shops.*

**Meats:** Serve a variety of cured meats such as prosciutto, sopressata, bresaola, salami, capicola, pepperoni, and mortadella. A word here about *salumi*: Although it is often confused with salami,

*salumi* is simply a term for Italian-style cured or preserved meat, mostly pork based. *Salumi* meats are salt-cured, smoked, and fermented and some, such as sausages and pâtés, are preserved in fat.

**Cheeses:** A range of good Italian cheeses is essential to an antipasto platter and they taste wonderful with salty meats, olives, and wine. Good choices include Asiago, Provolone, Parmesan, Robiola, mozzarella, or the small balls of mozzarella called *bocconcini.*

**Seafood:** You may want to serve some seafood in addition to the meat, cheese, and vegetables on the antipasto platter. Look for good-quality canned tuna and anchovies, and cooked and chilled squid, baby clams, and shrimp/prawns in the seafood section of the market or fish store. If you're up for cooking, prepare cold poached salmon or white fish, clams, and mussels on the half shell. Baked Clams with Walnuts & Herbs (page 103) and Chilled Mussels Vinaigrette (page 107) would be excellent additions to an antipasto platter.

**Vegetables:** Serve a wide range of raw and cooked vegetables to add color and texture to the platter. Red, yellow, and green bell peppers/capsicums; red and yellow cherry tomatoes; chopped fresh plum tomatoes; green/spring onions; and baby carrots drizzled with extra-virgin olive oil and sprinkled with some fresh herbs will look and taste terrific. Pickled and marinated vegetables, such as roasted peppers, pepperoncini, artichokes, cauliflower, and mushrooms available in jars, are also very tasty additions. Some other good fresh vegetables to cook and serve are steamed asparagus spears, artichokes, cauliflower, and green beans, roasted or grilled eggplant/aubergine, and zucchini/courgettes.

**Olives:** Serve a colorful array of olives to accompany everything on the platter.

**Breads:** Good bread choices are Italian baguettes and breadsticks, focaccia, ciabatta, and cheese straws. You may want to grill or toast small rounds of baguettes to make crostini.

Given the wide range of choices of high-quality Italian products that are available nowadays, it's very easy and fun to prepare and present a scrumptious and beautiful antipasto platter that your guests will enjoy feasting on. *Mangia!*

# mini empanadas with beef, green olives & raisins

**makes about 2 dozen hors d'oeuvres**

These savory little turnovers with hand-formed crusts and a luscious filling of ground/minced beef, raisins, and green olives are superb appetizers. You can make them up to a month ahead of time, as they freeze well. These are fantastic to eat with an Argentinean or Chilean red.

Dough:

2 cups/255 g unbleached all-purpose/plain
    flour, plus more for dusting

1 tbsp sugar

1 tsp salt

½ cup/115 g cold unsalted butter,
    cut into small pieces

2 large eggs, lightly beaten

1 tsp white vinegar

Filling:

1 tbsp corn or canola oil

1 small yellow onion, chopped

1 clove garlic, minced

½ lb/225 g ground/minced beef

¼ cup/40 g raisins

½ cup/70 g chopped green olives

½ tbsp tomato paste/puree

¼ cup/60 ml chicken stock or low-sodium broth

Kosher salt and freshly ground black pepper

Corn or canola oil for frying

To make the dough: Combine the flour, sugar, and salt in a food processor and pulse to mix. Add the butter and pulse until the mixture resembles coarse meal. Beat the eggs with 1 tbsp of water and the vinegar and drizzle over the flour mixture. Pulse until the dough just comes together. Turn out the dough onto a lightly floured work surface and knead gently until smooth, about 3 to 5 minutes. Wrap the dough in plastic wrap/cling film and refrigerate until firm, about 1 hour.

To make the filling: In a large skillet, heat the oil over medium heat. Add the onion and garlic and cook until the onion is softened, about 5 minutes. Add the beef to the pan and cook, breaking up the meat with a wooden spoon, until no pink remains, about 3 minutes. Add the raisins, olives, and tomato paste/puree and stir well. Add the chicken stock and simmer over moderate heat until the liquid has nearly evaporated, about 3 minutes. Season with salt and pepper. Let cool.

*continued*

Roll the dough out on a generously floured work surface to about ⅛ in/3 mm thick. Cut into 3-in/7.5-cm rounds with a floured biscuit cutter or glass, stamping out as many rounds as possible. Roll out any dough scraps and cut out additional rounds if possible. Brush the excess flour off the rounds.

Working with one round at a time and keeping the rest covered with plastic wrap/cling film, assemble the empanadas. Spoon about 2 tsp of the filling on one side of the dough round. Fold the dough over to enclose the filling and crimp the edges with a fork to seal. Cover with plastic wrap/cling film while you form the remaining empanadas.

Preheat the oven to 350°F/180°C/gas 4. Pour oil to a depth of about ½ in/12 mm into a skillet and heat until hot but not smoking. Working in batches, fry the empanadas, turning once, until browned and crisp, about 2 minutes per side. Drain on paper towels/absorbent paper and transfer to a baking sheet/tray. Keep warm in a low oven until all of the empanadas have been fried. Serve at once.

**Make-Ahead:** The filled, uncooked empanadas can be frozen on a baking sheet/tray, and stored in an airtight container for up to a month. Bake them, without thawing, in a 350°F/180°C/gas 4 oven for 20 to 25 minutes.

# cumin-scented lamb kebabs

**Makes 20 skewers; serves 6 to 8**

Fresh mint and oregano infuse succulent lamb in this fabulous grilled dish. When you're prepping the kebabs, be sure that the lamb pieces are bite-sized so that they can be eaten right off of the skewer. A full-bodied red wine like Cabernet Sauvignon is an excellent accompaniment here.

¼ cup/60 ml olive oil

2 tbsp chopped fresh oregano

1 tbsp chopped fresh mint

2 cloves garlic, minced

2 tsp ground cumin

1 tsp ground coriander

Pinch of cayenne pepper

Kosher salt and freshly ground black pepper

2 lb/910 g boneless leg or shoulder of lamb, cut into 1-in/2.5-cm cubes

Vegetable oil cooking spray for grilling

In a large bowl, stir together the olive oil, oregano, mint, garlic, cumin, ground coriander, cayenne, and salt and black pepper to taste. Stir in the lamb. Cover and let marinate in the refrigerator for at least 2 hours and up to 4 hours.

Soak 20 wooden skewers in cold water for at least 30 minutes. Meanwhile, prepare a medium-hot fire for direct grilling in a charcoal grill/barbecue, or preheat a gas grill to medium-high. Coat the grill rack with cooking oil spray to prevent sticking. Alternatively, preheat the broiler/grill.

Drain the skewers. Thread two lamb cubes on each skewer so they fill only half of the skewer, leaving the other half empty so you have a handle to work with.

Wearing an oven mitt or grill glove or using tongs, arrange the skewers directly over the fire. Grill, turning as needed, until browned and nicely grill-marked on all sides, about 6 minutes total for medium-rare. Or slip under the broiler/grill and broil/grill, turning as needed, until browned, about 6 to 8 minutes total.

Arrange the kebabs on a platter and serve at once.

# veal, pork & ricotta meatballs

**Makes about 3 dozen hors d'oeuvres**

Meatballs are fabulous and everyone has their own favorite recipe. Mine are made with veal, pork, and ricotta and Parmesan cheese. It's important to give them enough time to chill before cooking them. A classic pairing would be Chianti, as it always complements red meat and tomato sauce. A peppery, full-bodied Zinfandel also works well.

2 slices white country bread,
  crusts removed, cut into cubes
¾ lb/340 g ground/minced veal
¾ lb/340 g ground/minced pork
¾ cup/180 ml whole-milk ricotta cheese
¼ cup/30 g freshly grated Parmesan cheese

1 large egg, lightly beaten
1 tsp *fines herbes* or herbes de Provençe
Pinch of freshly grated nutmeg
Kosher salt and freshly ground black pepper
About ½ cup/120 ml olive oil for frying

Put the bread cubes in a food processor and pulse to make fine crumbs. Transfer to a large bowl. Add the veal and pork and mix together with your hands.

In another bowl, stir together the cheeses, egg, herbs, nutmeg, and salt and pepper to taste. Add the cheese mixture to the meat mixture and work the mixture together with your hands until it is well incorporated.

Roll the mixture into balls that are about 1 in/2.5 cm in diameter. Put them on a baking sheet/tray lined with parchment/baking paper. Refrigerate until well chilled, at least 4 hours or up to 2 days.

Heat the oil in a large sauté pan over medium heat. Add the meatballs to the pan, in batches, and cook until brown on one side before turning. Cook the meatballs, turning occasionally, until they are evenly cooked through, about 12 to 15 minutes. Drain on paper towels/absorbent paper and serve at once.

**Wine Bite Idea:**
For delicious deconstructed mini-meatball sandwiches, build skewers with a small square of Italian bread, a smear of tomato sauce, a meatball half, and a small piece of Parmesan cheese on each.

# kielbasa in red wine

**serves 6**

It's so interesting how a simple ingredient can change and enhance a dish. In this recipe, a bit of fresh orange zest adds a wonderful tangy flavor to ordinary kielbasa sausage. Chorizo sausage works very well here, too! This savory little bite requires almost no work and is excellent with a glass of Cabernet.

1½ lb/680 g kielbasa sausage
1 tbsp grated orange zest
½ cup/120 ml dry red wine

Preheat the oven to 400°F/200°C/gas 6.

Slice the sausage on the diagonal about ¾ in/2 cm thick. Spread the slices in a baking dish and bake until lightly browned, about 20 minutes.

Turn the sausages, sprinkle the orange zest over them, and pour in the wine. Bake 10 minutes longer. Serve hot or at room temperature.

# pulled pork sliders

**makes 16 sliders**

These delicious sliders are good to make when you want to serve something a bit more substantial than appetizers for a party. You'll need time for the pork to marinate in a dry rub—overnight is best—and time for slow cooking, so plan ahead. For the barbecue sauce, you can make your own, or use your favorite commercial brand. Many barbecue lovers feel that beer goes best with barbecue, but slightly chilled Rioja or Barbera taste mighty fine with pulled pork, too.

1 pork roast (3 to 4 lb/1.4 to 1.8 kg),
    preferably pork shoulder or Boston butt

1 tbsp olive oil

Dry Rub:

3 tbsp paprika

1 tbsp kosher salt

1 tbsp granulated sugar

1 tbsp brown/demerara sugar

1 tbsp ground cumin

1 tbsp chili powder

1 tsp cayenne pepper

Freshly ground black pepper

Barbecue Sauce:

1 tbsp corn oil

1 small yellow onion, finely chopped

2 cloves garlic, thinly sliced

1½ cups/360 ml ketchup/tomato sauce

¾ cup/180 ml cider vinegar

½ cup/100 g firmly packed brown/demerara sugar

2 tbsp chili powder

1 tbsp Dijon mustard

Dash of hot-pepper sauce

16 slider (mini hamburger) rolls
    or 8 regular hamburger rolls, split

Pat the pork dry and brush with the olive oil.

To make the dry rub: In a small bowl, stir together the paprika, salt, both sugars, cumin, chili powder, cayenne, and black pepper to taste. Rub the dry rub all over the pork, wrap in plastic wrap/cling film, and let marinate in the refrigerator for at least 4 hours or up to overnight.

Preheat the oven to 300°F/150°C/gas 2. Put the pork on a rack in a large roasting pan/tray and roast until an instant-read thermometer registers 170°F/80°C, about 6 hours.

*continued*

To make the barbecue sauce: Heat the corn oil in a saucepan over medium heat. Add the onion and garlic and sauté until softened and golden, about 5 minutes. Add the ketchup/tomato sauce, vinegar, brown/demerara sugar, chili powder, mustard, and hot-pepper sauce and stir to mix well. Simmer gently, stirring occasionally, until the sauce thickens and the flavors blend, 20 to 25 minutes. Taste and adjust the seasoning, if necessary.

Remove the pork roast from the oven and transfer to a cutting board or large platter. Tent loosely with aluminum foil and let rest for 15 to 20 minutes. "Pull" the pork apart with two forks to form shreds and transfer to a large bowl. Add the sauce to the shredded pork.

Spoon the pulled pork onto the bottom halves of the rolls, dividing it evenly. Replace the tops of the rolls; if using regular hamburger rolls, cut each sandwich in half. Serve at once.

# serving tapas

*The ritual of eating tapas with wine comes from Spain. It is said that serving tapas started in bars in Andalusia, where pieces of bread topped with ham or cheese were placed over wineglasses (tapa means "cover") to keep fruit flies away from the sweet wine. A delightful way to eat, drink, and enjoy evolved from these humble beginnings.*

*A tapas party is an easy and wonderful way to bring your friends and family together. A spread of earthy Spanish delicacies—cured meats, seafood, cheeses, olives, nuts—and a few dishes prepared in advance are all you need to get the party rolling. Look for authentic Spanish foods in specialty markets and gourmet shops. There are also a number of sources, such as the Spanish Table, La Tienda, and Despana, for ordering Spanish specialties online.*

*Good wines to serve with tapas are crisp, dry white Albariño; sparkling Cava; or for reds, Tempranillo or Rioja. Chilled dry sherry is also a good match, as it is the traditional partner for tapas.*

Here are some suggestions for serving tapas:

**Meats:** Serve paper-thin slices of Serrano ham (*jamón serrano*) or *jamón Iberico*, along with chunks of spicy chorizo sausage.

**Fish:** There are a number of excellent Spanish seafoods that are available in tins and jars. Octopus, anchovies, white anchovies (*boquerones*), and sardines are all good choices. Excellent cooked seafood dishes include sautéed shrimp/prawns with garlic, Chilled Mussels Vinaigrette (page 107), and Fish & Avocado Ceviche (page 111).

**Cheeses:** Spanish cheeses such as Manchego, Cabrales, and Mahon are fantastic, and they are virtually essential to a Spanish tapas platter. Serve them at room temperature.

**Olives and Nuts:** Look for rich and meaty Spanish olives such as Manzanilla, Arbequina, and Empeltre. Delicate and delicious Marcona almonds are a real treat, especially after they're roasted and salted. They're also good for stuffing into dates with a sliver of Manchego or Cabrales cheese and wrapping with Serrano ham.

**Vegetables:** Some good choices are steamed or roasted asparagus spears wrapped in thin slices of Serrano ham; Spanish potato and vegetable salad; and marinated *piquillo* peppers.

**Cooked Dishes:** A few good cooked dishes that will round out the tapas platter include Manchego Quesadillas with Roasted Red Peppers & Onions (page 48), Grilled Manchego Cheese & Serrano Ham Sandwich Bites (page 87), Mini Empanadas with Beef, Green Olives & Raisins (page 133), and Chorizo in Red Wine (a variation of Kielbasa in Red Wine, page 137).

*Chapter 9*

# SMALL SWEETS
# & TREATS

Delicious Last Bites & Sips
of the Evening

# caramelized fruit with goat cheese

**serves 6 to 8**

This is a lovely way to serve a range of seasonal fruits. For a springtime menu, make this recipe with apricots; use ripe peaches, plums, or nectarines in summer; and tangy goat cheese really meets its match with fresh figs, which have a short ripeness season running from mid-summer to the fall, depending on your region. This simple and elegant dessert bite is quite delicious with a Sauvignon Blanc or Muscat wine.

6 fresh apricots, peaches, plums, or nectarines,
   cut in half lengthwise and pitted,
   or 6 fresh figs, cut in half lengthwise
½ cup/100 g sugar
½ cup/60 g fresh goat cheese, at room temperature

Preheat the broiler/grill.

Dip the cut sides of the fruit into the sugar and put them on a baking sheet/tray, cut-side up. Broil/grill the fruit until caramelized, 1 to 2 minutes. Remove and let cool a bit. Top each fruit half with a spoonful of goat cheese and serve at once.

# fresh fruit with mascarpone cream

**serves 8 to 10**

A platter of fresh fruit makes a beautiful dessert presentation, especially when it's served with a bowl of luscious mascarpone cream for dipping. You can add other fruits to the plate such as fresh peaches, plums, nectarines, and berries, depending on what's ripe and in season. A Riesling or Moscato D'Asti would pair very nicely with the fruit and mascarpone.

⅓ cup/75 g mascarpone cheese

1 tbsp sugar

½ tsp pure vanilla extract

⅔ cup/165 ml plain yogurt

6 assorted firm but ripe pears,
 cored and cut into eighths

6 assorted apples, cored and cut into eighths

2 lb/910 kg mixed green and red grapes, stemmed

Whisk together the mascarpone cheese, sugar, and vanilla. Add the yogurt and stir until smooth. Cover and refrigerate until well chilled, at least 1 hour and up to 2 days.

Arrange the pears, apples, and grapes on a large platter with a bowl of the mascarpone cream and serve.

# blondie bites

**makes sixteen 2-in/5-cm or sixty-four 1-in/2.5-cm squares**

Blondie bites, full of pecans, are irresistible. Cut into small squares and serve with toothpicks. A glass of Vin Santo or Tawny port would be lovely to drink with these.

½ cup/115 g unsalted butter

1 cup/200 g firmly packed brown/
   demerara sugar

2 large eggs, at room temperature

1½ tsp pure vanilla extract

1 cup/130 g cake/soft-wheat flour
   (not self-rising/self-raising)

¼ tsp salt

⅓ cup/40 g chopped pecans

Preheat the oven to 350°F/180°C/gas 4. Butter an 8-in/20-cm square baking pan.

Combine the butter and sugar in a large bowl. Beat with a hand mixer until fluffy, 2 to 3 minutes. Add the eggs, one at a time, blending well after each addition. Stir in the vanilla. Add the flour and salt and beat until well mixed. Fold in the pecans. Pour the batter into the prepared pan and smooth the top.

Bake in the center of the oven until a cake tester comes out clean, 30 to 35 minutes. Let cool in the pan before cutting into squares.

**Make-Ahead:** To store the blondies, put them in an airtight container separated by sheets of wax/greaseproof paper.

# mini apple-walnut pies

**Makes 12 mini pies**

These individual pies are baked in a muffin tin instead of a pie pan and they're a lot of fun to make and serve during the autumn apple season. I like to use a mix of sweet and tart apples, such as McIntosh and Granny Smith. Riesling or sparkling wine pairs nicely with the pies.

Pastry Dough:

1 cup/130 g unbleached all-purpose/
   plain flour

½ tsp salt

5 tbsp/70 g cold unsalted butter,
   cut into pieces

1½ tsp vegetable shortening/lard, chilled

4 tbsp/60 ml ice water, or as needed

Filling:

4 tbsp/55 g unsalted butter

2 Granny Smith apples, peeled, cored, and diced

2 McIntosh apples, peeled, cored, and diced

¾ cup/150 g firmly packed brown/demerara sugar

¾ tsp ground cinnamon

¾ tsp freshly grated nutmeg

¼ tsp ground ginger

¼ tsp salt

1 cup/115 g chopped walnuts

Whipped cream or crème fraîche for serving (optional)

To make the pastry dough: In a food processor, combine the flour, salt, butter, and shortening/lard and pulse four or five times. With the machine running, slowly add 2 or 3 tbsp of the ice water. The dough should begin to mass on the blade. If not, add another 1 or 2 tbsp water a drop at a time, just until the dough holds together. Do not overmix.

Turn the dough out onto a lightly floured work surface. Flatten it with the palm of your hand, dust lightly with flour, and wrap the dough in plastic wrap/cling film. Refrigerate until chilled, 1 or 2 hours.

Preheat the oven to 425°F/220°C/gas 7.

*continued*

Roll out the dough ⅛ in/3 mm thick on a clean lightly floured work surface. Using a knife or a biscuit cutter, cut out circles about 5 in/12 cm in diameter. Line a standard 12-cup muffin tin with the dough circles, letting the extra dough hang over the edge of each cup. Bake the pastry shells for 10 minutes, then remove from oven and reduce the oven temperature to 350°F/180°C/gas 4.

To make the filling: In a large skillet, melt the butter over medium heat. Add the apples, brown/demerara sugar, cinnamon, nutmeg, ginger, and salt. Cook, stirring, until the sugar is melted and the apples are well coated, 2 to 3 minutes. Add the walnuts and continue to cook until about 2 minutes more. Remove from the heat.

Spoon the filling into each pastry shell. Bake until golden brown, about 25 to 30 minutes, being careful that the crust doesn't burn. Serve the pies warm or at room temperature, with a dollop of whipped cream, if desired.

**Make-Ahead:** The pies can be made a few hours ahead of time. Reheat in a low oven for about 20 minutes before serving.

# chocolate-cherry cookies

**makes about 4 dozen cookies/biscuits**

Try these terrific dark chocolate bites with a cup of espresso or a glass of full-bodied red wine or port.

2¼ cups/280 g unbleached all-purpose/
   plain flour

1 tsp baking soda/bicarbonate of soda

Pinch of salt

1 cup/225 g unsalted butter,
   at room temperature

½ cup/115 g vegetable shortening/
   lard, at room temperature

1½ cups/300 g granulated sugar

½ cup/100 g firmly packed light brown/
   demerara sugar

1 tsp pure vanilla extract

2 large eggs, at room temperature

1½ cups/255 g semisweet/
   plain chocolate chunks

½ cup/85 g dried cherries

Preheat the oven to 375°F/190°C/gas 5.

Combine the flour, baking soda/bicarbonate of soda, and salt in a medium bowl and set aside. In a large bowl, beat the butter, shortening/lard, both sugars, and vanilla until smooth. Add the eggs, one at a time, incorporating well after each addition. Stir in the flour mixture, chocolate chunks, and dried cherries. Drop by rounded teaspoonfuls onto ungreased baking sheets/trays.

Bake until golden brown, 10 to 12 minutes. Let cool on the sheets/trays for about 2 minutes, then transfer to the wire racks to cool completely.

**Make-Ahead:** To store the cookies/biscuits, put them in an airtight container separated by sheets of wax/greaseproof paper.

# dark chocolate mousse

**serves 6 to 8**

A rich chocolate mousse, flavored with espresso and lightened with whipped cream, is a nice dessert to serve at the end of the evening. It's also great for entertaining because it can be made a day ahead of time. Many wine aficionados love to drink a glass of Cabernet Sauvignon or old-vine Zinfandel with a dark chocolate dessert.

6 oz/170 g bittersweet chocolate, finely chopped (about 1 cup)

4 large eggs, at room temperature, separated

2 tsp sugar

½ cup/120 ml espresso or strong-brewed coffee

⅔ cup/165 ml heavy (whipping)/double cream

Fresh strawberries, raspberries, blackberries, or blueberries for garnish (optional)

Whipped cream for garnish (optional)

Melt the chocolate in the top of a double boiler set over barely simmering water, stirring until smooth. Set aside to cool slightly.

In a bowl, using an electric mixer set on medium speed, beat the egg yolks and sugar until pale yellow. Stir in the chocolate and espresso until well mixed.

In another bowl, with the mixer set on high speed, whip the cream with a wire whip or beater until it forms stiff peaks. Using a rubber spatula, gently fold it into the chocolate mixture.

In a clean, dry bowl, beat the egg whites at high speed with a clean, dry whisk or clean beaters until stiff peaks form. Using a rubber spatula, gently fold into the chocolate mousse, taking care to incorporate the whites thoroughly.

Spoon the mousse into a large serving bowl or individual dessert bowls, ramekins, or goblets. Put in the refrigerator until well chilled, at least 4 hours or up to overnight. Serve garnished with berries and whipped cream, if desired.

# pairing wine with sweets

*A glass of dessert wine served with coffee and a sweet can be the perfect finale to a convivial evening of eating and sipping. There is a wide range of dessert wines to choose from and that pair well with favorite desserts, and others that are delicious to drink on their own and act as dessert itself (some do beautifully either way). Here are a few suggestions for wines to drink with desserts. Let your palate and your pocketbook be your guide.*

• White Rieslings and Gewürztraminers from Germany, California, and Washington state are very good to drink with pies, crisps, and tarts.

• Chocolate lovers swear by slow sipping old-vine Zinfandel or full-bodied Cabernet Sauvignon with all manner of chocolate desserts, from cake to mousse to truffles.

• Rich and golden Vin Santo from the Tuscany region of Italy is wonderful to savor on its own and it is *the* dessert wine to serve with biscotti for delicious dunking.

• Domestic *moscato* (Muscat wine) from California or sweet and sparkling Moscato d'Asti from Italy are fantastic when paired with creamy desserts such as crème brûlée, flan, or mousse. They're also terrific with a mild hard cheese or goat cheese and walnuts.

• Ice wine that is produced primarily in Canada is quite sweet and while many prefer to drink it on its own, it's a good accompaniment to fruit tarts and a number of blue cheeses.

• Vintage ports from Portugal go well with a range of desserts from cakes, pies, and cookies to dark chocolates and fresh fruit. Tawny port is wonderful to have on hand during the holidays since it pairs beautifully with pecan and pumpkin pies as well as aged Cheddar and Stilton cheeses.

• Sherry from Spain has a deep, full-bodied flavor and is another good accompaniment to holiday desserts and fruit and cheese platters.

# acknowledgments

My thanks and gratitude go out to the people who worked with me on this book:

Kate Mathis for her incredibly beautiful food photography.

Adrienne Anderson, kitchen whiz extraordinaire, for her wonderful food styling.

Marcus Hay, for his prop styling and brilliant vision.

Amy Thompson from Lucy's Whey in Chelsea Market, for her excellent cheese advice and selections.

Angela Miller, my agent, who helped make this book happen, and who taught me a lot about goat cheese.

The people at Chronicle Books, especially Bill LeBlond, who helped me develop the idea for this book over a glass of rosé at Bar Boulud, and to Sarah Billingsley, for her editorial support and for keeping the book on track.

My cooking pals, Philip Hoffman, Susan Kramer, Bernard Scharf, Carol Bokuniewicz, John Smallwood, Liz Trovato, Charlie Clough, Lynn Edelson, Michael Principe, Cathy Medwick, and Jeffrey Silberman, with whom I've shared many dinners, a few glasses of wine, and great times over the years.

My family, Lester, Zan, and Isabelle, for always being there for me and for everything else.

# index

Note: Page references in *italics* refer to photographs.